San Francisco

Compact Guide: San Francisco is a culture-based guide for a culture-based destination, revealing the beauty of the city's architecture, the wealth of its museums and the delights of its streets and squares.

This is one of more than 80 titles in *Apa Publications'* new series of pocket-sized, easy-to-use guidebooks intended for the independent-minded traveler. *Compact Guides* are in essence travel encyclopedias in miniature, designed to be comprehensive yet portable, as well as up-to-date and authoritative.

Star Attractions

An instant reference guide to some of San Francisco's most popular attractions to help you on your way.

Market Street p16

Chinatown p18

Telegraph Hill and Coit Tower p21

Fisherman's Wharf p22

Transamerica Pyramid p29

Alcatraz p34

Golden Gate Bridge p42

Alamo Square p45

Museum of Modern Art p26

Golden Gate Park p39

Monterey's Cannery Row p53

San Francisco

Introduction

Places

Culture

Leisure

Practical Information

San Francisco – America's Favorite City

Opposite: the Golden Gate Bridge opened in 1937

Of all the cities in the US, San Francisco has long been a favorite in the hearts and minds of newcomers to the West. Around 150 years ago, the city was the springboard for the famous '49ers, those pioneers in the vanguard of the Gold Rush; in this century it became the focal point for student protests, the beatniks and the gay movement. During the 1960s, the 'City by the Bay' became a symbol of rebellion for America's youth, a city of love and freedom – an image that the city still lives with and one that it would not want to lose. Despite the post-modern office blocks and forward-looking high-tech industries of nearby Silicon Valley, there is still a certain nostalgia for the flower children.

It's an enchantingly beautiful city, one of the most distinctive in the world, with its gorgeous panoramas from 43 different hills, watery vistas, a verdant park that seems to go on forever and the mostly lowscale development dominated by old houses that delight the eye just as they did when they were built a century or more ago. It's also a city with a strong sense of neighborhood, each with a distinct identity and yet overlapping and inter-relating, so people mix and mingle and go through them instead of bypassing them on the highway when they want to visit some other part of town. It's easy to see why this is America's favorite metropolis.

And one more thing: do not shorten those evocative words San Francisco to 'Frisco. For all inhabitants and true admirers, it is simply The City.

Location and size

San Francisco lies at the northern end of a hilly peninsula between the Pacific Ocean and San Francisco Bay, a long, sheltered Bay some 40 miles (60km) in length that forms the biggest natural harbor in the US. The only link between the Bay and the open sea is the Golden Gate, the narrow straits only 1 mile (1.6km) wide which serve as the western gateway to California.

Geologically speaking, this opening in the otherwise unbroken coast mountains owes its existence to the San Andreas fault *(see page 9)*, which has been responsible for the many earthquakes that have struck this coastal region.

The foothills of the coast mountains block off the sea on both sides of the Golden Gate. To the north, it is the hills of Marin County, to the south, the 43 hills on which San Francisco stands, including Twin Peaks (908ft/277m and 902ft/275m), Nob Hill (373ft/114m), Russian Hill (295ft/90m) and Telegraph Hill (249ft/76m).

Haight-Ashbury hippy shop

The Golden Gate refers to the straits between the Bay and the sea

5

Flower power, 1990s style

6

Coastal walks are commonplace

The Embarcadero

With a total area of only 46 sq.miles (120sq.km), San Francisco is very small when compared to its national importance. The distance across the peninsula from the ocean to the Bay is only 10 miles (15km) as the crow flies. Downtown, together with the Financial District and Chinatown, Nob Hill, South of Market and North Beach, can easily be covered on foot in about two hours. Then, it is a straightforward journey of a mile or two by bus or taxi to the nearby districts of Haight-Ashbury, Castro, Mission and Golden Gate Park.

San Francisco is really just the name for the main settlement in the Bay Area. Fringing the Bay is an unbroken line of towns, some little known, but some, like San Jose, even bigger than San Francisco itself. The 1.6-mile (2.7-km) long Golden Gate Bridge crosses over the straits to the north, while to the east is the San Francisco-Oakland Bridge. To the south lies high-tech, high-profile Silicon Valley.

Climate and when to go

Mark Twain once remarked: 'The coldest winter that I have ever experienced was a summer in San Francisco'. Although he was exaggerating, most West Coast residents will recognize the phenomenon. The Pacific Ocean is cold, and even in summer the water temperature rarely exceeds 62°F (17°C). When it heats up on land, the coast is subject to fog. From June to August, it rises up in the early morning like a gray wall, creating dramatic scenes around the Golden Gate Bridge. Sometimes it clears by noon, sometimes not at all, but many unsuspecting tourists arrive without a warm sweater and are caught unaware by the mists and the cold, moist breeze.

Visitors often find the months of September to November and March to May much more pleasant than the

middle of summer. The warmest month is, in fact, September when the average daytime temperature reaches 73°F (23°C). The coldest month is January but even then the mercury rarely falls below 55°F (13°C). Snow almost never falls in this mild maritime climate.

The busiest time in the museums and at the main tourist sights is around Easter and from June to October. Although rain is frequent during the winter, it is often T-shirt weather in the city, even in January. Winter is a good time to visit, especially for anyone interested in the excellent skiing in the Sierra Nevada mountains.

Population

Few cities conform better to the term 'multi-cultural' than San Francisco. Less than half its 724,000 residents were born in the US, and over 100 different languages can be heard, but English is the common denominator. Newspapers and magazines are published in 31 different languages. Around 32 percent of San Franciscans have European ancestors and 28.6 percent are Asiatic, with half of these Chinese. Central and South America account for 13.3 percent, 10.6 percent are African-Americans, and 3.6 percent are Native Americans.

San Francisco is only the fourth largest city in California, but the densely populated area around the Bay is home to about 6.4 million people. This puts it in fourth place in the US, after New York, Los Angeles and Chicago.

Nature and the environment

Nature is never far away in San Francisco. As well as the city's own fine parks and scenic areas, just 12 miles (20km) to the north are the mighty redwood trees of Muir Woods National Monument *(see page 47)*. To the south, the rocky Pacific Coast is wild and secluded.

San Francisco Bay has been a haven for flora and fauna for thousands of years. The plankton that forms in the marshland on the edge of the Bay and the shoals of tiny fish have provided nourishment for many different types of aquatic birds and the gray whales of the Pacific. For several years, local researchers have been working on alternative energy sources. On the road from suburban Oakland eastward, huge wind farms with thousands of turbines testify to the success of their efforts.

Economy

Trade and finance made San Francisco great, and the city's unique natural harbor is still an important center for today's Asia-bound cargo ships, although the giant port complex at Oakland now handles most of the goods. The Bank of America, Wells Fargo Bank, California First Bank and the Bank of California plus many insurance companies

Performance perfection

Nature is never far from the city

The redwoods of Muir Woods

have their headquarters in the Financial District, which is also home to the most important stock exchange on the West Coast.

In recent years, however, tourism has accounted for the biggest proportion of San Francisco's economy. About 8 million tourists come to the city every year, spending almost $4 billion. One in six workers depend on the tourist trade for their livelihood. More than 10 percent of the working population are employed in restaurants or hotels.

Many local high-tech firms have become major players on the international scene. The excellent colleges around the Bay – Berkeley and Stanford are two of the four universities in the San Francisco area – have produced first-rate engineers and technical and scientific researchers. Computer companies such as Apple, Sun Microsystems and Hewlett-Packard are based here, together with countless smaller chip and software manufacturers. Genetic research and biotechnology companies are also attracted to the region. Of all the organizations and laboratories in the world researching these branches of science, some 30 percent are to be found in the San Francisco Bay area.

Politics and administration

For administrative purposes, the city is divided into 11 postal zones with five-figure zip codes, all beginning with 941. The much bigger Bay Area comprises the nine counties of Alameda, Contra Costa, Marin, Napa, San Francisco, San Mateo, Santa Clara, Solano and Sonoma.

The city is run by a mayor and a Board of Supervisors. San Francisco has seen several of its politicians nominated for posts at national level; Mayor Dianne Feinstein, for example, was elected to the US Senate in 1992.

The gay movement

The city's substantial gay community is proud of its self-confidence, its history and its political success. Although no-one can be sure of the exact figure, there are thought to be well over 100,000 gays in San Francisco.

The tolerant attitude that prevails in the city might well have its origins in the Gold Rush era. During the mid-1800s, in the city's red light district, the Barbary Coast (*see page 19*), there were several bars where homosexuals were welcomed. Later, during World War II, some of the soldiers who had been discharged from the army for their homosexuality stayed on in San Francisco, and during the 1950s homosexuals sought refuge in this liberal enclave from McCarthyite anti-gay purges.

At that time, the Castro District was a predominantly Irish-Catholic quarter, but at the beginning of the 1970s important changes took place. The rents in Haight-Ashbury, the hippy district, began to rise, so the gays and les-

Silicon Valley is an influence

Academy of Sciences

Fairie Queen candy, the Castro

bians living there were forced to look for cheaper accommodation in the neighboring Castro District.

Castro Street underwent rapid changes as cafés, bars, restaurants, bookshops, theaters and political centers opened up, and in time the entire district came to embody the gay scene. The Gay Movement, started in the 1950s, began to achieve considerable political success, with gays taking up elected seats in the city government. No longer were homosexuals just another fringe group, but an important part of the city, with considerable economic and political clout.

The big one

San Francisco is built on unsteady ground directly above the notorious San Andreas fault which marks the dividing line between two huge sections of the earth's crust, the Northern Pacific and the North American plates. The Northern Pacific plate is sliding past the North American plate in a northerly direction at the rate of 1.6 to 2.4 inches (4 to 6cm) a year, causing occasional large earthquakes to originate near the surface along the path of the fault. Every year, hundreds of minor tremors are recorded, not just along the principal fault line that runs in the vicinity of San Francisco, but also along many other minor geological faults.

Once or twice every century, a 'big one' rocks California. In 1906 the last earthquake to exceed 8.0 on the Richter scale devastated San Francisco. The California quakes in 1989 and 1994 were less disastrous. Buildings are usually able to withstand quakes of up to 7.0. Many seismologists believe that the 'big one' is yet to come, probably sometime during the next 120 years. Inhabitants have come to terms with the risk. There is no apocalyptic mood, but in San Francisco people tend to enjoy every day, perhaps because they know it could be their last one.

Loud and proud

The theater is an area landmark

9

View from Twin Peaks

Aftermath of the 1906 earthquake

Historical Highlights

35,000 to 12,000BC Nomadic tribes from Asia cross the frozen Bering Straits.

1,000BC Indians who revere the earth strive for a society in harmony with the physical environment in the area known today as San Francisco.

AD 500 Miwok Indians settle in the San Francisco Bay region and live on fish, venison and acorn flour.

1542 João Rodriguez Cabrillo, a Portuguese explorer in the service of the Spanish king, sails from Mexico along the Pacific Coast. He discovers San Diego Bay, but misses the narrow inlet to San Francisco Bay, probably because of the summer fog. Further expeditions in search of new lands and gold follow in the 16th and 17th centuries.

1579 The English explorer and buccaneer, Sir Francis Drake, anchors off Point Reyes, north of present-day San Francisco, and sends several landing parties ashore.

1769 In order to secure the Spanish claim to California, an expedition heads north from Mexico. The vanguard under José Ortega discovers San Francisco Bay.

1776 Juan Bautista de Anza and 30 soldiers reach the northern tip of the peninsula and build a fortress, the forerunner of today's Presidio. The accompanying Franciscan *padres* found the Dolores Mission, California's sixth mission station, several miles inland. The *padres* hear of gold from the Indians but keep silent on the matter for fear of unwelcome visitors.

1821 Mexico and its colony of California declare independence from Spain. The missions are later secularized. Large *ranchos* are formed, including that of the Swiss exile, Johann August Sutter, near Sacramento.

1824 The Mexican Congress promises security to law-abiding foreign settlers. American and English businessmen begin a gradual influx. William Richardson, an Englishman, is widely acknowledged as the person who founds Yerba Buena, the town preceding San Francisco.

1846 The US goes to war with Mexico. American settlers declare California an independent republic and in Sonoma on the northern side of San Francisco Bay they hoist the new state flag (still in use) showing a picture of a grizzly bear.

1846 Yerba Buena is renamed San Francisco by the American settlers.

1848 On January 2, after defeat in the war, Mexico signs the Treaty of Guadaloupe Hidalgo and cedes California to the US. A few weeks later, gold is discovered by the contractor James Marshall on Sutter's ranch in the Sierra Nevada. The Gold Rush begins.

1849 Thousands of prospectors flock to California in search of gold. 30,000 from mainland US arrive by covered wagons and San Francisco is the main port of entry for the 40,000 people who sail from Europe, Australia, South America and China. Numbers are swelled by a further 9,000 prospectors from Mexico. The local economy booms, but it is shopkeepers, not miners, who make the most money.

1850 California is admitted to the Union. San Francisco's population rises to 50,000.

1859 As the Gold Rush ends, silver is discovered in the mountains of Nevada. San Francisco is again the main supply depot and develops from a prosperous frontier town into a metropolis.

1860s The Chinese population grows rapidly. Immigrants come initially to mine, but their success brings resentment, and they are sent away from the richest veins.

1869 The first transcontinental railroad is completed, with a terminus at Oakland by San Francisco Bay. Track construction is carried out by thousands of Chinese laborers, who later settle in San Francisco. This is the beginning of the city's Chinatown quarter.

1870s Rich businessmen, lawyers and speculators who profit from the mines live and entertain in high style on Nob Hill, creating a different class of citizens from the rough fortune hunters of the old pioneer town.

1871 Golden Gate Park is established.

1873 The world's first cable cars trundle up and down the city's steep hills, between Kearny and Jones streets.

1880s Despite the corruption of the railroad magnates, cultural life flourishes with California State and San Francisco universities, public and private libraries, 12 theaters and an opera house at the Tivoli.

1906 At 5.12am on Good Friday, April 18, an earthquake measuring 8.2 on the Richter scale rocks San Francisco. The central business district, Nob Hill and Chinatown are destroyed. Damage amounts to $500m and 250,000 people are left homeless. Reconstruction on an enormous scale soon begins.

1914 The opening of the Panama Canal has a huge impact on the city, as it is no longer necessary for vessels from the West to make the long journey around Cape Horn. World War I boosts mining, manufacturing and agriculture. Abundant oil reserves are mined. The economy is buoyant.

1915 The city celebrates the end of the rebuilding scheme with the Panama Pacific Exposition. San Francisco's Thomas Watson receives the very first transcontinental phone call from Alexander Graham Bell.

1929 Striking dock-workers paralyze the city. The unemployed line up outside soup kitchens.

1934 Labor troubles culminate in the General Strike, when the International Longshoremen's Union immobilize traffic in the port.

1937 The Golden Gate Bridge is opened to an uproarious reception, six months after the Oakland Bay Bridge.

1941 onwards World War II sees the influx of more than 500,000 workers in response to new industries in the Bay Area, in addition to thousands of soldiers and sailors passing through to the war in the Pacific or stationed around the Bay. With the government fearing sabotage, Japanese-Americans are incarcerated and sent to mass internment camps.

1945 Delegates from all over the world meet in San Francisco for the San Francisco Conference, which establishes the United Nations. 50 members sign the United Nations Charter.

1951 Prime Minister Yoshida of Japan signs the treaty ending World War II at Opera House.

1953 Counter-culture groups across the US have started to congregate in the city. Lawrence Ferlinghetti opens his North Beach City Lights bookstore, which becomes the hang-out for the 'Beats', or beatniks.

1955 The US's first lesbian group, the Daughters of Bilitis, is formed, the first instance of homosexuals banding together as a pressure group.

1966–71 Golden Gate Park and the nearby Haight-Ashbury district become the focal point of the hippy movement. The Black Panther movement is formed in Oakland. Students at Berkeley form the Free Speech Movement, protest against the war in Vietnam and become the vanguard of radicalism.

1974 The BART (Bay Area Rapid Transit System) starts a regular transportation service.

1978 Mayor George Moscone and Harvey Milk, a city supervisor and spokesperson for homosexuals, are shot by Dan White, an enraged former member of the Board of Supervisors. The lenient sentence imposed on White leads to the massive gay 'White Night' riots which gain worldwide attention.

1980s AIDS hits the San Francisco gay community. As more and more cases as diagnosed, numerous self-help organizations are founded.

1989 A serious earthquake measuring 7.1 on the Richter scale hits San Francisco. Sixty-nine people die and damage runs to billions of dollars.

1995 The opening of the spectacular Museum of Modern Art marks the climax of San Francisco's new building boom.

1996 The area known as SoMa (South of Market Street) spearheaded by the Museum of Modern Art, attracts thousands of visitors to its galleries, cafés and clubs.

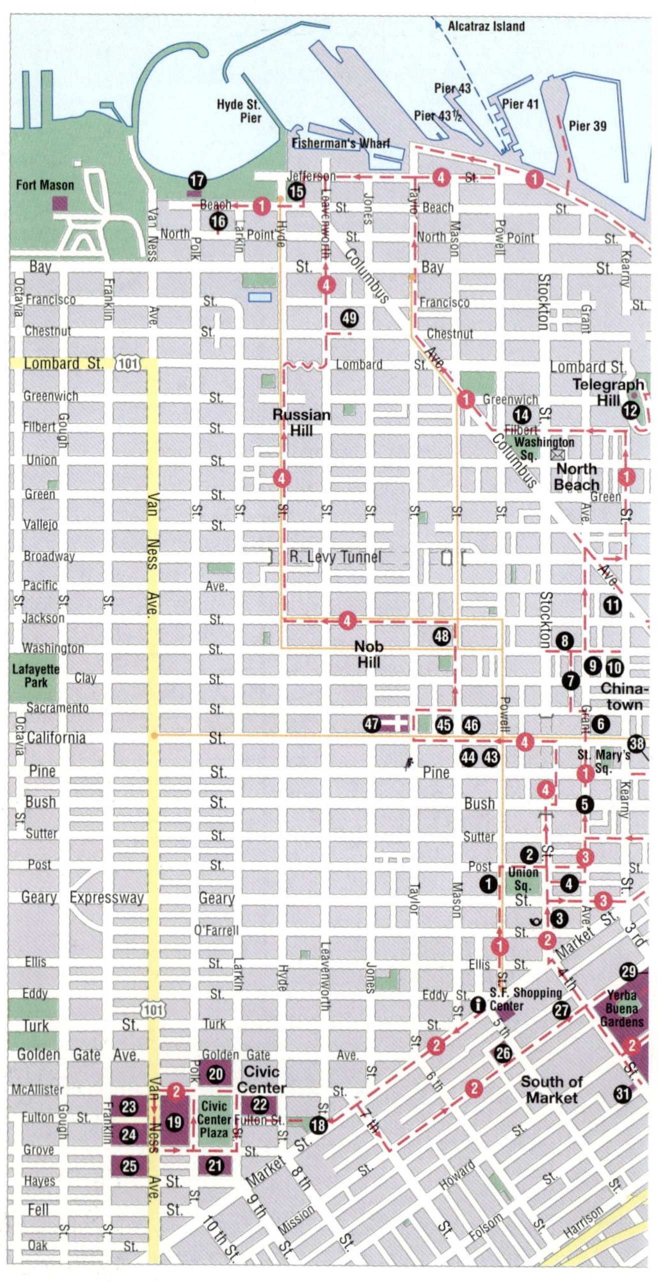

Alcatraz Island
Pier 43
Pier 43½
Pier 41
Pier 39
Hyde St. Pier
Fisherman's Wharf
Fort Mason
Jefferson St.
Beach
North Point
Bay
Francisco
Chestnut
Lombard St. 101
Greenwich
Filbert
Union
Green
Vallejo
Broadway
Pacific
Jackson
Washington
Lafayette Park
Clay
Sacramento
California St.
Pine
Bush
Sutter
Post
Geary
Expressway
O'Farrell
Ellis
Eddy
Turk
Golden Gate Ave.
McAllister
Fulton
Grove
Hayes
Fell
Oak
Van Ness Ave.
Octavia
Franklin
Gough
Polk
Larkin
Hyde
Leavenworth
Jones
Taylor
Mason
Powell
Stockton
Grant
Kearny
Columbus Ave.
Russian Hill
R. Levy Tunnel
Nob Hill
Telegraph Hill
North Beach
Washington Sq.
Filbert St.
Greenwich
Chinatown
St. Mary's Sq.
Union Sq.
S.F. Shopping Center
Yerba Buena Gardens
South of Market
Civic Center
Civic Center Plaza
Market
Mission
Howard
Folsom
Harrison
3rd St.
4th St.
5th St.
6th St.
7th St.
8th St.
9th St.
10th St.
Fulton St.
Beach
North Point
Chestnut
Francisco
Bay
Stockton St.
Green St.
Point St.
Jefferson St.

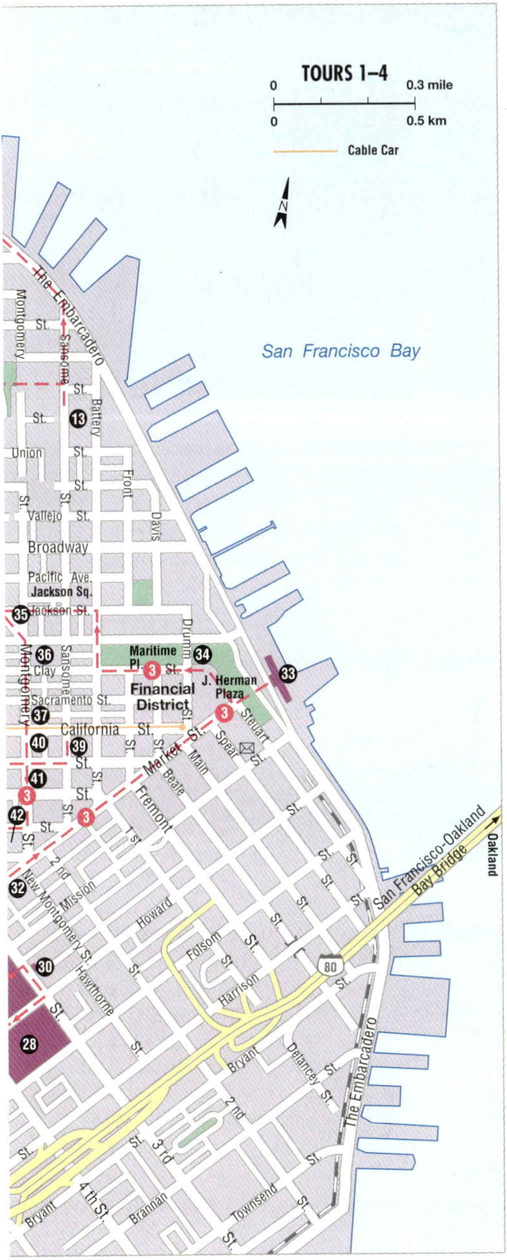

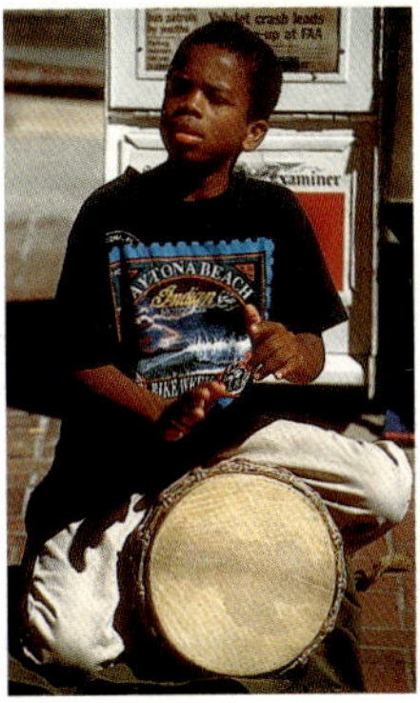

TOURS 1–4

0   0.3 mile
0   0.5 km

—— Cable Car

N

San Francisco Bay

The Embarcadero
Montgomery St.
Sansome
Battery St.
13
Union St.
Front
St.
Davis
St.
Vallejo St.
Broadway
Pacific Ave.
Jackson Sq.
Jackson St.
35
36 Clay
Montgomery
Sansome
Maritime Pl
34
Drumm
33
Financial District
J. Herman Plaza
Sacramento St.
37
California St.
40 39
Market St.
Steuart St.
Spear St.
Main
41
42
3
Fremont
Beate
1st St.
32
New Montgomery St.
Mission
Howard St.
30
Hawthorne
Folsom St.
Harrison St.
28
80
San Francisco–Oakland Bay Bridge
Oakland
The Embarcadero
Bryant
2nd
Delancey St.
St.
3rd
4th St.
Brannan
Townsend St.

Tin How Temple, Chinatown p18

15

Music on Market Street p16

Tour boat to Alcatraz p34

Tour 1

16

Heart of the City

Market Street – Union Square – Chinatown – North Beach – Telegraph Hill – Washington Square – Fisherman's Wharf *See map on pages 14–15*

This walk is perfect for first-time visitors to San Francisco as it takes in most of the main tourist sights. The tour can be completed in one day, but you may prefer to break it up into smaller sections and spread it out over a number of days. If time allows, think about taking one of the boat trips around the harbor that depart from Fisherman's Wharf. A car would be more of a hindrance than a help, but you will need sturdy shoes, as the steep streets of San Francisco can inflict painful blisters on the underprepared.

Start out from **Market Street**, San Francisco's main artery that cuts across the city from the northeast to the southwest. The **San Francisco Visitor Information Center** is situated on the lower level of **Hallidie Plaza** at the corner of Powell Street and Market. As well as city maps and brochures, MUNI passes *(see page 69)* for the cable cars and city buses are available from here. The departure point for the cable cars is at the same junction. Even early in the morning a long line usually forms at the terminal, so it's an idea to walk the first part of the tour and leave the cable cars until later.

Union Square acquired its name at the beginning of the 1860s, when it was the venue for pro-Union sympathizers during the Civil War. The 100-ft (30-m) granite obelisk in the middle of the palm-shaded square was erected in

Market Street and (below) Union Square

1903 by President Theodore Roosevelt to commemorate the American navy's victory over the Spanish fleet off Manila in 1898. The **Westin St Francis Hotel** ❶ on the west side of the square is another legacy from the turn of the century. The wealthy Crocker family, who made their fortune from the railroad, had this mansion built in 1904 in Italian Renaissance style. The handsome, restored lobby with its Corinthian columns demonstrates clearly the grandeur of San Francisco's old hotels. Scenes from Dashiell Hammet's *The Maltese Falcon* were set in this hotel. Hammet himself supposedly spent time here while an investigator for Pinkertons, the private detective agency.

The side streets to the north of the St Francis are home to numerous art galleries, high-class boutiques and exclusive antique shops. Some of the smaller, newly renovated 1920s hotels are also situated here.

Saks Fifth Avenue occupies the north side of Union Square next to the 36-story **Grand Hyatt Hotel** ❷. If you are disappointed by this rather sober-looking building, the fountain at the entrance on Stockton Street may compensate: its designer, Ruth Asawa, has created miniature bronze replicas of many of the city's main tourist sites.

At the southeast corner of the square is **Neiman Marcus** ❸. Built in 1982, it replaced San Francisco's first department store, the City of Paris, built by the Verdier merchant family of Paris. The architects of the newer building, Philip Johnson and John Burgee, were obliged to incorporate the magnificent glass dome of the original store into their design. It retains the Parisian coat-of-arms with its motto *Fluctuat nec mergitur* or 'It swims but will never sink' – an appropriate statement for a city as vulnerable to earthquakes as San Francisco.

Follow **Maiden Lane** ❹ from Stockton Street on the east side of Union Square. It is not difficult to guess how this narrow alley received its name. During the tough Gold-Rush era, men came here to look for female company. Now it is an attractive pedestrianized zone lined with cafés, an ideal place to pause for cappuccino or lunch. Just a few yards further on at No. 140 stands an architectural gem. In 1948 Frank Lloyd Wright created this building as the model for his designs for the Guggenheim Museum in New York – complete with spiral staircase. It is now an art gallery.

At the junction of Maiden Lane and Grant Avenue, the green roofs of **Chinatown Gate** ❺ appear. This photogenic entrance was presented to San Francisco in 1970 to bring good luck. It is the job of the guard dog to keep the evil spirits away, while the dolphins on the roof promise prosperity. The snaking dragons on the roof ridge (it is often called the **Dragon Gate**) bring good luck to all those who pass beneath it.

Maiden Lane

Dragon Gate, Chinatown

Bicycle tri-shaw boys

Buddhist temples on Waverly

★★★ **Chinatown**, a compact district of barely 20 streets between Stockton Street and Kearny Street, is home to more than 70,000 Chinese, and is thought to be the biggest Chinese settlement outside Asia. Grant Avenue, the area's main street, is heavily commercialized, but it is worth wandering down some of the side streets past the little workshops, tiny restaurants and shops selling jade jewelry, herbs, strange looking fruit, herbs and medicinal ointments. Chinatown is extremely atmospheric. The clatter and jangle of a thousand different tongues speaking Chinese mingles with the sounds of bells, windchimes and vendors hawking their wares. Steam pours out from restaurants selling noodles and dim sum, while the butcher shops have strange and exotic animals dangling in their front windows.

Grant Avenue was laid out around 1835 by the whaling captain, William Richardson. At the northeast corner of Grant Avenue and California Street stands the reddish-brown, almost 100ft (30m) high tower of **St Mary's Church ❻**, one of the oldest Catholic churches on the West Coast. Built in 1854 by Chinese workers, it was for a long time regarded as a sanctuary against the immorality of the nearby bars and brothels. **St Mary's Square** lies a few yards to the east. This little park is an interesting spot first thing in the morning, when, in front of Beniamino Bufano's metal statue of the first president of the Chinese republic, Sun Yat-Sen, the residents of the district often perform *tai chi* exercises.

Return to Grant Avenue. Two blocks further on make a detour into the short, and once highly disreputable **Waverly Place ❼**, which runs parallel to Grant Avenue. Buddhist temples, some dating from the years just after the 1906 earthquake, occupy the upper floors of the narrow houses. Although not very well signposted, three of them are open to visitors: **Norras Temple** (no. 109), **Tien How Temple** (no. 125) and **Jeng Seng Temple** (no. 146). Simply climb the steep stairs to just below the roof and the temple attendants will allow you to enter. Depending on their mood and also their English, these custodians will explain the significance of the red and gold altars, the symbolism and the sacrificial offerings. The temples are situated on the top floor for one simple reason: there should only be a roof between the Buddha and heaven, so nobody is allowed to live above the deity.

Take a stroll along the narrow lanes around Waverly Place and, if time permits, seek out **Old Chinatown Lane ❽**, a little further up, off Washington Street. This picturesque, dead-end road once had a reputation as a street of sin and it is still used by Hollywood movie directors as a setting for sinister scenes. Behind it runs **Stockton Street**, which today is what Grant Avenue used to be, namely Chinatown's main shopping street, full of every-day shops where residents buy their provisions.

Return via Washington Street and Grant Avenue to one of the most attractive sights in the area, the pagoda-style **Bank of Canton ❾**. This bright-red, lavishly decorated house with a three-story roof was built in 1906 and, until 1949, was a telephone exchange. Unlike many Chinese, the telephonists who worked here were well paid, as they had to cope, not only with various Chinese dialects, but with all the names of their 2,000 or so customers.

On the next corner is **Portsmouth Square ❿**, a square that was the plaza for the Spanish village of Yerba Buena and the center of San Francisco at the time of the Gold Rush. It was from here on May 11, 1848 that news of the discovery of gold in the Sierra Nevada was proclaimed. This historic soil – above a huge underground car park – is now where the children of Chinatown play. On the tables in the upper section of the square, you can watch old men enjoying a game of *mah-jong*, while in the north-west corner stands a statue of Robert Louis Stevenson, the author of *Treasure Island*. He lived in San Francisco around 1880 and spent many afternoons here. A small **Chinese Culture Center**, where exhibitions of contemporary art take place, is housed on the second floor of the Holiday Inn Hotel.

Return to Grant Avenue and follow the remaining streets of Chinatown on to ★★ **North Beach**, the Italian district around Columbus Avenue. First impressions can be misleading. Neon signs for peep shows and sex shops warn that this is the 'red light district' of San Francisco, the last remnant of the notorious Barbary Coast, where seafarers drowned their sorrows in cheap dives before embarking, often for good, on a ship to Shanghai (hence the

Child's play

Old men engaged in mah-jong

19

North Beach street artists

Bohemian life in North Beach

The beat goes on

term 'shanghaied'). Such practices have long since disappeared and with the imminent departure of many of the naval crews currently stationed in the city, the red lights will soon be going out. But around Columbus Avenue and in the neighboring streets, the atmosphere of little Italy will continue to prevail: noisy bars, little *trattorias* and *osterias*, clattering pizza ovens and hissing espresso coffee machines. In the 1930s, as many as 60,000 Italians lived in the North Beach area. Cheap wine, dingy cafés, good food and the Mediterranean atmosphere attracted the intellectuals and the students of life. This Bohemian atmosphere lasted for many years, and two decades later the 'Beat Generation', personified by writers such as Jack Kerouac, moved into the neighborhood to practice (and publicize) their unconventional lifestyles. Kerouac wrote his classic *On the Road* while in San Francisco, and Allen Ginsberg (of *Howl* fame), Neal Cassady and Gregory Corso met to drink and talk in the cafés and bars of North Beach. These 'beatniks' incurred the wrath of Middle America, as they were seen to be rebelling against the prevailing social norms. And indeed they were, paving the way for the youth movements of the 1960s, the hippies of Golden Gate Park and the Berkeley student protests.

Only a few yards from the junction of Grant Avenue and Columbus Avenue on the right-hand side is the **City Lights Bookstore** ⓫, which, under the management of its founder Lawrence Ferlinghetti – himself an author and poet – published the main works of the Beat Generation writers. Founded in 1953, the bookshop became an intellectual hothouse for the movement, and even today it is still a rendezvous for the city's writing fraternity. The little street which crosses Columbus Avenue was in 1988 renamed **Jack Kerouac Street**, a belated recognition of the literary contribution of this one-time rebel.

Other popular haunts from the Beat Generation have also survived. **Tosca Café** (242 Columbus Avenue), is famous for its special cappuccino laced with brandy. The **Vesuvio** bar, next door to the City Lights Bookstore, was for several years the meeting place for North Beach's intelligentsia. It is said that Jack Kerouac once drank himself senseless here and so missed a get-together with fellow writer Henry Miller in Big Sur – the two never did meet.

Columbus Avenue, laid out in 1873, cuts diagonally across North Beach. Look out for **Monari's Deli** on the corner of Vallejo Street; it has been here since 1896 and has changed very little. The church of **St Francis of Assisi** opposite was built in 1860. Destroyed in the 1906 earthquake, it was faithfully restored in 1913.

Take a look up at the huge Transamerica Pyramid *(see page 29)* at the southeastern end of Columbus Avenue and then retrace your steps to follow Broadway eastwards. One block further on, turn into **Kearny Street**, a steep incline that is typical of the scenes in the *Streets of San Francisco*. With every step, the view back over the city gets better and better: it is worth the effort to climb to the very top.

From ★★ **Telegraph Hill** (300ft/90m) a spectacular view opens out across San Francisco Bay, taking in the harbor, the city and the Golden Gate Bridge. From the summit, a heroic statue of Christopher Columbus, a gift to the city from the Italian community, looks down over the Bay. When a telegraph mast was erected on the summit in 1853 to inform the townsfolk of vessels approaching the Golden Gate, it was named Signal Hill, later to be changed to Telegraph Hill. In 1890 a large wooden entertainment palace was erected at the top of the hill with access via a cable railway. The restaurant and dance hall were initially very popular, but they burned down 13 years later and were not rebuilt.

Columbus stands on Telegraph Hill

Since 1933, the top of Telegraph Hill has been occupied by 223-ft (68-m) ★ **Coit Tower**. This stylish structure stands as a monument to the wealthy widow, Lillie Coit, who wanted to pay her respects to the fire brigade for their bravery during the 1906 earthquake. When she died in 1929, she bequeathed a sum of money for the construction of a memorial on Telegraph Hill. Some citizens were opposed to the erection of a bland concrete tower, but during the Depression it was hard to reject any project that provided work. The architect, Arthur Brown Jr, also designed San Francisco's City Hall *(see page 24)*. Twenty-five artists painted the interior walls in Mexican social-realist style, paid with funds awarded by California's work creation program. Depicting scenes from everyday life, the paintings vividly illustrate the economic hardships of life in the 1930s.

21

While there are fine views of the Financial District and central city area from the forecourt, it's well worth taking the elevator up to the **viewing platform**, from where the vista is magnificent.

Coit Tower and mural

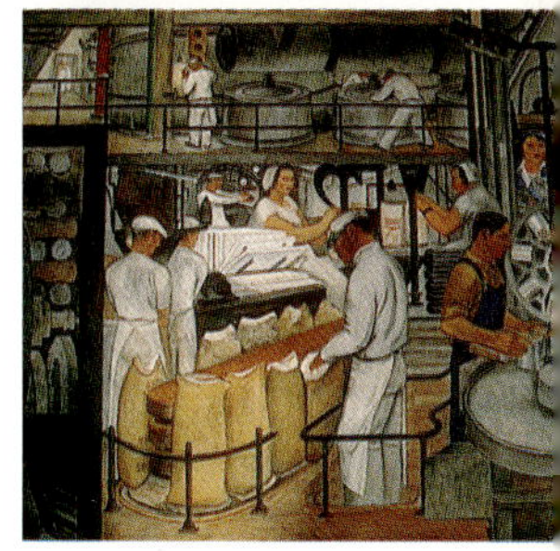

There are two possible routes from Telegraph Hill down to the harbor and Fisherman's Wharf. Shorter, steeper paths lead down the **Greenwich Steps** or **Filbert Steps** on the east side of the hill, providing fine views of the city as well as glimpses of some of its oldest buildings. The old steps wind down through a residential area bedecked with attractive flower hedges and past ramshackle wooden cottages, which once provided poor artists with a cheap roof over their heads. Ironically, this district is now one of the most desirable in San Francisco. Wooden flights of steps once criss-crossed the hillsides everywhere, but many fell victim to fire after the 1906 earthquake. It is said

Piering into the distance

Washington Square

Seafood by the Bay

that the steps on Telegraph Hill did not succumb because the Italian residents stayed behind to fight. If water was not available, they dowsed the flames with red wine. The steps end at **Levi's Plaza** ⑬, an extensive, but rather nondescript complex named after Levi Strauss, the inventor of the famous blue jeans. One of Strauss's ancestors still runs the international company from its headquarters here.

The second, slightly longer route from the top of Telegraph Hill leads first along Filbert Street through the old Italian quarter to the west and then to **Washington Square**. Laid out in 1862, the grassy section of this large square was used in 1906 as a camp-site for the hundreds of people whose homes had been destroyed by fire. Lillie Hitchcock had a second monument erected here to remember the fire-fighters, but it bears no comparison with the tower on Coit Hill. The statue shows three firemen in action. Perhaps of more interest is the church of **St Peter and Paul** ⑭ on the north side of the square. The snow-white building with its two pointed towers was built between 1922 and 1927 in neo-Gothic style and financed by the area's Italian business and fishing community. Every year on a Sunday in October a procession of fishermen carries a statue of the Virgin Mary down to the harbor to have their boats blessed. From here, it is a short walk via Columbus Street and Taylor Street to one of San Francisco's main tourist attractions.

Well before the turn of the century, ★★★ **Fisherman's Wharf** was the center of the fishing industry. Nowadays, just a few dozen fishing boats use the pier for business, but there is still plenty to see and do. Souvenir shops and fish restaurants line the **Embarcadero** and some of the old piers. Mime artists and other street performers demonstrate their skills in return for small change.

At busy stalls by **Piers 41** and **43**, departure points for boat tours of the harbor and **Alcatraz** *(see page 34)*, traders sell prawn cocktails, mussel soup and freshly cooked crabs, not to mention the appetizing sourdough bread *(see page 59)*, which is one of San Francisco's specialties.

One of the most popular spots by the water's edge is further west: **Pier 39**, boasting numerous restaurants and bars, an old carousel and lots of tourist shops.

Pier 39 is also home to some larger attractions. At the start look for the ultra-modern **Underwater World aquarium**, where you can watch fish swimming in a long glass tunnel. A movie about San Francisco is shown on a large screen at the **Cinemax Theater**, while on the stage at the end of the pier, skillful acrobats and street artists entertain the passers-by. Another attraction is the huge colony of **California sea lions** that have established themselves on large wooden platforms in the harbor. It is possible to watch these elegant 6-ft (2-m) long creatures at close quarters, but be warned: their noisy barking drowns out any conversation.

Other tourist places, such as waxworks and freak shows, can be found by continuing westwards, but an alternative route is through the two shopping centers, both formerly industrial sites: **The Cannery** ⑮ on Jefferson Street, a beautiful old fruit-packing plant converted into a lavish three-story complex in 1967, and **Ghirardelli Square** ⑯ on Beach Street. The latter, an imposing red-brick structure, was once a chocolate factory owned by the Italian immigrant Domenico Ghirardelli. He arrived in the US in 1850 and, between 1893 and 1916, worked with his sons to build up the factory. Old chocolate-making machines, some of which are still in working order, can be seen in the clock-tower.

If you are interested in the seafaring history of the Pacific Coast, make a point of visiting the ★★ **Maritime Museum** ⑰. Housed in an Art Deco structure that bears a remarkable resemblance to a boat, it contains a large number of wonderful model ships, historic photos, maps and other memorabilia. A number of carefully restored vessels are moored alongside **Hyde Street Pier**, also part of the museum, and they are open to visitors both above and below deck. The two jewels in the collection are the *Balclutha*, a three-mast sailing vessel which was made in Glasgow in 1886 and was one of the last boats to sail the Cape Horn route, and the schooner, *C.A. Thayer*, which was used to transport timber along the northwest coast around the turn of the century.

To return to Market Street from Fisherman's Wharf, take the **Powell-Hyde Line** cable car from the **Cable Car Turntable** at the foot of Hyde Street.

Ghirardelli Square

23

Composing by The Cannery

Maritime Museum

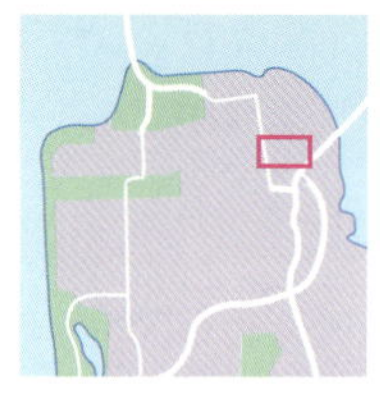

UN Plaza

Civic Center

City Hall

Tour 2

South of Market Street

Market Street – Civic Center – Yerba Buena Gardens – San Francisco Museum of Modern Art – Union Square *See map on pages 14–15*

Two bright faces of San Francisco feature in this short stroll around Market Street. On the one hand, there is the grand federal building complex comprising City Hall and its huge dome while, on the other, the revitalized South of Market area by the old harbor, now the center of the city's cultural scene. You could complete this tour in two hours but if you want to linger in the museums and galleries, it will take a whole day.

UN Plaza ⓲, a broad concourse for the Civic Center flanked by trees and fountains, is situated just off Market Street. This spacious, classically inspired Beaux Arts style complex is not just San Francisco's administrative headquarters, but also the home of the city's opera and symphony orchestra. At the turn of the century the mayor commissioned the Chicago architect, David Burnham, to basically redesign the city. In 1905 Burnham, who had studied in Paris, produced a bold plan based very closely on the French capital. Like Place de l'Etoile, the Civic Center would be the focal point for a series of broad boulevards radiating outwards, but in the end, only this particular part of the project came to fruition.

Towering above the **Civic Center Plaza** is ★ **City Hall** ⓳, one of the most beautiful public buildings in the country. The dome, modeled on St Peter's in Rome, weighs 90,000 tons. It was designed in 1912 by Arthur Brown Jr, another graduate of the Paris Ecole des Beaux Arts, who also worked on the Opera House, Coit Tower and Berkeley City Hall. Other grand elements of the complex surround the great square in front of City Hall: the **State Office Building** ⓴ on the north side and, opposite, the **Bill Graham Civic Auditorium** ㉑, renamed in 1992 after the impresario who managed several Bay Area rock groups during the 1960s. The hall is used for exhibitions and concerts. On the east side stands the seven-story former **Public Library** ㉒. The old library, which dates from 1917, is due to be renovated in the next few years and will become the new home of the Asian Art Museum *(see page 41)*.

Take a look behind the City Hall at the **War Memorial Group**, two buildings finished in 1932 with identical Beaux-Arts facades. On the right-hand side stands the **Veterans Auditorium Building** ㉓, built in 1932 as a memorial to the dead of World War I and housing the 915-seat **Herbst Auditorium**; on the left, the **Opera House** ㉔ with its nationally acclaimed company. Wagner's *Ring Cycle* is performed at regular intervals. The building is probably more famous, though, as having been the venue for the foundation of the United Nations. On July 26 1945, 43 countries signed the United Nations Charter in a ceremony on the opera house stage.

The modern glass and stone facade next door belongs to the **Louise M. Davies Symphony Hall** ㉕, home of San Francisco's symphony orchestra. Opened in 1980, the hall contains the biggest concert organ in the US – it boasts 9,235 pipes.

Return to the city center along Market Street or, better, on **Mission Street**, which runs parallel. To the south lies the **South of Market** (**SoMa**) district, a part of the city which has experienced a new lease of life. Boutiques, cafés and trendy shops have burgeoned recently, but many of the historic buildings, such as the old **US Mint** ㉖ have survived the changes. Here, in this massive structure (1875), silver from Nevada was first converted into dollars and then stored in huge safes in the cellar.

The small **Cartoon Art Museum** ㉗, a few yards further on, will prove to be a source of much amusement. Themed exhibitions retell the history of comics from their early beginnings. Children will particularly enjoy the comic playroom (closed Monday and Tuesday).

Right by 4th Street, ★ **Yerba Buena Gardens** is an oasis of green in a busy part of the city. You may find it hard to resist taking a break on one of the park benches amid the lawns and flowerbeds which lie just to the north of the **Moscone Convention Center** ㉘. The waterfall in the park was built as a memorial to Martin Luther King.

Davies Symphony Hall

Yerba Buena Gardens

25

Moscone Convention Center

Museum of Modern Art

Center for the Arts

Plays, modern art exhibitions and experimental multimedia performances are staged in the **Center for the Arts** ❷❾ along the eastern side of the park.

The arts continue on the other side of 3rd Street. Opened in 1995, the spectacular ★★ **San Francisco Museum of Modern Art** ❸⓿, cost $60 million and was designed by the Swiss architect Mario Botta. It is worth stepping inside this post-modern building, if only to admire the sunlight effects in the entrance hall beneath the five-story glass-roofed staircase. But many visitors also come here to admire one of the West's finest art collections.

Works by American and European expressionists such as Max Ernst, Picasso, Paul Klee and the Californian painter Richard Diebenkorn are exhibited on the first floor. The second floor consists of the architecture and design sections and also stages special touring exhibitions. Fascinating displays of experimental 1920s and 1930s photography can be found on the third floor, while the fourth floor is devoted mainly to contemporary works of art. Be sure to leave enough time to visit the museum shop and the steel and chrome café.

Camera buffs should make a short detour to the ★ **Ansel Adams Center for Photography** ❸❶. There is not a lot of room, but some wonderful examples of photographic art are displayed here. Ansel Adams was a master of Absolute Realism, who, during the 1930s, produced fine black and white landscape photographs of the US, particularly the Southwest and Yosemite National Park. Together with the F/64 photographic group, he believed in portraying natural detail and set many standards which remain valid today. The museum exhibits works by Adams himself, as well as traveling exhibitions of modern photography. The postcards and posters on sale in the small shop make good souvenirs.

Tour 3

Downtown and the Financial District

Union Square – Market Street – Ferry Building – Embarcadero Center – Financial District – Union Square
See map on pages 14–15

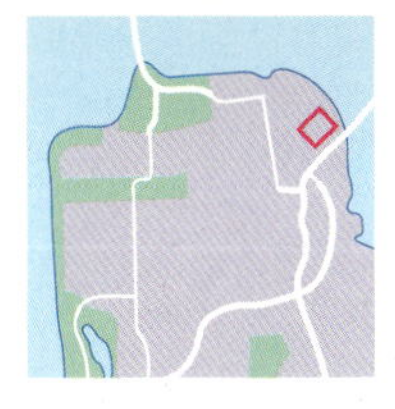

Unlike their colleagues in New York or Chicago, for many years the bankers and managers of San Francisco did not work in tall skyscrapers. The risk of earthquakes was too great; the earth beneath the banks was simply too unsteady. But civil engineers have now learned how to construct quakeproof buildings, and this tour takes in the buildings that dominate today's San Francisco skyline: the Bank of America, the Embarcadero Center and the Transamerica Pyramid. At lunch-time you can rest your legs and enjoy the view from the ferry across to Sausalito on the north bank of San Francisco Bay. If you include the boat trip, then the walk will take the whole day, otherwise only three to four hours.

Set out from **Union Square** *(see page 16)* towards the east, passing the boutiques of Geary Street (named after the mayor of San Francisco at the time of the Gold Rush). Down on **Market Street**, turn left. This main road through the city center leads straight to the Bay, with the ferry building tower visible in the distance. On the right-hand side at the junction with New Montgomery Street stands one of San Francisco's oldest hotels, the ★ **Sheraton Palace** ㉜. Dating originally from 1875, it was first owned by William Ralston, the founder of the Bank of California. The internal decor could not be more extravagant: Italian marble everywhere, plus the finest porcelain from France and Bavaria. This 700-room hotel soon became one of the most famous in the world and certainly the place to stay when in San Francisco. It was here that Enrico Caruso narrowly escaped death on the morning of the 1906 earthquake, swearing that he would never return to the city again. The hotel burned to the ground after the quake, but was rebuilt shortly afterwards. Worth seeing is the **Garden Court**, a huge domed room with marble pillars, crystal chandeliers and mirrored walkways that now serves as the hotel's dining room.

Market Street cuts through the city from the southwest to the northeast

Walk to the end of Market Street, or, if you prefer, ride in one of the city's street cars. Despite their age – the tracks date from the 1950s – these beautiful vehicles are one of San Francisco's more recent acquisitions. Cities throughout the country donated their obsolete historic carriages, which were then lavishly restored and put into service covering a route that goes from the Ferry Building to the Cas-

Oakland Bay Bridge

Villaincourt Fountain

Hyatt Regency atrium

tro District. An extension of the track alongside the harbor to Fisherman's Wharf is planned.

This part of Market Street is a text book of architectural history: modern glass towers alternate with historic industrial edifices such as the **Hobart Building** (1914) on the corner of Market Street and Montgomery Street, the magnificent Art Deco **Shell Building** (1929; 100 Bush Street) and the terracotta-clad **PG&E Building** (1945; 245 Market Street).

Market Street's highpoint is the **Ferry Building** ❸, designed in 1898 by A. Page Brown as a grand gateway to the city. Based on Seville's Giralda bell-tower in Spain, this fine structure with two wings pierced by arcades was located at the city's busiest site at the turn of the century; at its height, some 50 million passengers passed from sea to land through the terminal each year. Every 15 seconds, a cable car left the Ferry Building to take new arrivals into the city center, but when the **Oakland Bay Bridge** was opened in 1936, the Ferry Building lost its importance.

Ferries to the northern half of the Bay now leave from here and, if the weather is fine, it is well worth taking a boat trip on one of the Golden Gate Ferries across to ★ **Sausalito** *(see page 47)*. The crossing provides an excellent view over the city's skyline and you can stop off for lunch in one of Sausalito's fish restaurants.

Return to the Ferry Building and head towards the **Embarcadero Center** ❸, a large complex of six, modern skyscrapers which extend over four long blocks. This city-within-a-city was built between 1971 and 1981 by John Portman and Associates, who built similar complexes in New York, Chicago and other cities. The center includes two hotels as well as a shopping area with 150 stores and restaurants spread over three levels.

The **Justin Herman Plaza** on the east side is a busy spot at lunchtime as the elegantly dressed office workers from the Financial District gather to eat their sandwiches and gossip. Street musicians and the sound of splashing water from the **Villaincourt Fountain** create a soothing atmosphere. The futuristic fountain, known locally as 'Ten on the Richter Scale', has been at the center of controversy, as water spraying from stone blocks conjures up images of a post-earthquake scene. The most impressive structure in the Embarcadero Center is the soaring, John Portman-designed ★ **Hyatt Regency Hotel**.

It is no accident that San Francisco is one of the country's most important financial centers. The growth of the city's **Financial District** was spawned during the Gold Rush, when the city's original shoreline began to burgeon. The first banks were established in **Montgomery Street**,

Financial District

still the main street for the banking fraternity. To the north stands one of its most impressive symbols, the ★★ **Transamerica Pyramid** ㊱. Reaching a height of 850ft (260m) and with 48 floors, it is the highest building in San Francisco. When it was built in 1972, it caused much controversy. Many residents felt that it spoiled their beautiful city, while purists regarded the plans by William Pereira Associates as typical of crazy Californians. But the work went ahead and it is now impossible to imagine the city without the pyramid's distinctive spire dominating the skyline. For many adherents of modern architecture, the pyramid has acquired almost cult status.

Carry on along Montgomery Street and you will come across the headquarters of two other banks, both of which enjoy a prominent place in the history of the West Coast. One, **Wells Fargo** ㊲, conjures up images of stagecoaches and frontier ambushes, but the founders, Henry Wells and William Fargo, set up the company in Montgomery Street during 1852 to transport mail and provisions to the mining outposts in the Sierra Nevada mountains. Their business soon expanded into a bank with the movement of gold their specialty. Mergers with other banks during the 20th century has created one of the country's most important credit institutions. The history of the company is documented in the **Wells Fargo History Room**. Some of the original stagecoaches, old shotguns, safes and banknotes are among the displays.

Only a few yards further, on the corner of California Street and Kearny Street, stands the massive headquarters of another prominent financial organization, the **Bank of America** ㊳. When it was completed in 1969, the bank's 52 floors made it the tallest building in the city and the biggest bank in the world. The story of the Bank of America is a classic rags-to-riches tale. In 1904 its founder, Amadeo P. Giannini, opened the Bank of Italy, a credit

Transamerica Pyramid

29

Wells Fargo Bank

Lunchtime, Justin Herman Plaza

Businessman in bronze

Crocker Galleria

company for penniless immigrants who had been refused help from other banks. Giannini's lending policy proved extremely successful and he gradually bought up other banks. By 1930 the Bank of America, as it had become, was one of the biggest banks in the country. On the top floor of the building, the elegant **Carnelian Room** offers a tremendous view over the city. Well worth a closer look is the black marble sculpture outside the foyer. Strictly speaking, it is called *Transcendence*, but many prefer to describe it as the 'Banker's Heart'.

Other new skyscrapers rise up from the nearby side streets. The top 11 floors of the 48-story **First Interstate Center ❸**, built in 1987, are occupied by the top-class Mandarin Hotel. Other notable buildings on Montgomery Street include the **Kohl Building ❹**. Constructed in 1901, this was one of the first attempts to build a high-rise block and it now looks rather tame. Nevertheless, it did withstand the 1906 earthquake thanks to its steel girder construction. This architectural style remained the fashion for multi-story buildings until the 1920s.

The **Mills Building ❹** at the junction of Montgomery Street and Bush Street was designed in 1892 by architects from the notable Chicago Architects' School and has some interesting Romanesque features. Note the neo-Gothic decorations on the facade of the **Russ Building** opposite. When it was finished in 1927, it became the city's tallest building. If you return to Union Square via Sutter Street, you will pass another architectural gem, the **Hallidie Building** (1917; 130 Sutter Street). Fire escapes and ornamental metal frames decorate its glass frontage. You may well be tempted inside the modern, glass-domed **Crocker Galleria ❹** opposite, which was opened in 1982, so round off this tour with a stroll past the upscale shops that make up most of its three levels.

Tour 4

The Steep Streets of San Francisco

Union Square – Nob Hill – Cable Car Barn – Russian Hill – Lombard Street – Alcatraz *See map on pages 14–15*

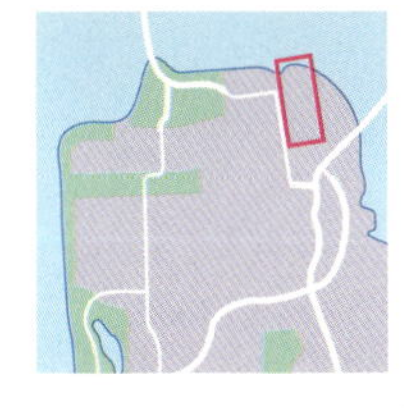

What better way of exploring San Francisco than by cable car? If you make the trip to Alcatraz, this tour will take a full day, otherwise you will need only about three hours.

Leave **Union Square** via the **Hyatt Hotel** with its pretty fountain and follow Stockton Street northwards along the edge of Chinatown – do not pass through the Stockton Tunnel, but use the steps to one side. The hustle and bustle of downtown San Francisco quickly disappears and you are soon surrounded by old mansions, many of them owned by wealthy lawyers, and the wonderful Ritz Carlton Hotel. By California Street turn left and start the uphill climb, or jump on one of the passing cable cars to the top of ★ ★ ★ **Nob Hill**.

Cable car descending Nob Hill

When the cable car line was opened in the 1870s, this area around the 340-ft (103m) high hill became very popular with San Francisco's richest residents. Stanford, Crocker and Hopkins, the millionaires behind the construction of the transcontinental railroad, were among the first to build houses on Nob Hill. Robert Louis Stevenson described the district as a 'millionaire's slum'. The derivation of the name Nob Hill is ambiguous. A 'knob', of course, is an old word for a hill, but 'nob' is also a shortened version for 'nabob', meaning 'a very wealthy man'.

Cable customers and brakeman

Most of the magnificent houses around Huntington Park fell victim to the fires which followed the 1906 earthquake, but many of the properties were rebuilt. Only the granite walls of the former Victorian villa that belonged to Leland Stanford now remain visible in front of the **Stanford Court Hotel ㊸**. This magnificent palace built by the railroad king had several reception rooms and even a winter garden, where the plants could be lowered by electricity. The present Stanford Hotel dates from 1911 and was extensively renovated in 1972.

A colleague of Stanford, Mark Hopkins, built his home next door. It was designed by Hopkins' wife and was thought to be the most exclusive residence on Nob Hill. The wooden building and an extensive art gallery were destroyed by fire in 1906. In its place stands the **Mark Hopkins Hotel ㊹** (1925), a worthy successor with a lobby of marble columns. Situated at the top of the hotel is the famous revolving restaurant, the **Top of the Mark**, and it is well worth taking the elevator for a cocktail or even a swank meal. The views of the city are magnificent.

The only surviving pre-earthquake building on Nob Hill is the **Flood Mansion** ㊺. Dating from 1886, this miniature castle belonged to the night-club owner James Flood. Designed by an English architect in Italian Renaissance style, it had 40 rooms. The sandstone structure survived the great fire relatively unscathed and the mansion is now home to the exclusive Pacific Union Club.

Opposite, one of the oldest and most famous hotels in San Francisco, the **Fairmont** ㊻ also fell victim to the flames. The daughter of the real estate shark 'Bonanza' James G. Fair, started work on the project in 1902, but costs began to exceed the heiress's resources. It stood unfinished for four years, but in 1906 a buyer was found. Then it burned to the ground after the earthquake. In 1907 the hotel was finally opened. One of its attractions is undoubtedly the fine view over the city from the **Crown Room** bar. This bar, set in a tower that was added later, is reached via a glass elevator. The grand hotel portal and foyer are often seen in movies and TV series.

A few yards further on along California Street, on the west side of Huntington Park, stands one of the biggest edifices on Nob Hill: the **Grace Cathedral** ㊼. This 355ft (108m) long, neo-Gothic church, which bears a remarkable similarity to Notre Dame in Paris, is the seat of the bishop of the Episcopal Church. Before the earthquake, the site was occupied by a mansion belonging to the banker and art expert, William Crocker, son of the railroad magnate, Charles Crocker. Although his collection of paintings was saved from the flames, the house burned down and the family donated the land to the church. Work on the huge cathedral, part of which is made from quakeproof reinforced concrete, began in 1910 and ended in 1964. The portals, cast from Lorenzo Ghiberti's *Gates of Paradise* from the baptistry in Florence, are worth a closer look.

Return to the Fairmont Hotel and two blocks further north, on the corner of Mason Street and Washington Street, is the **Cable Car Barn** ㊽, a museum as well as a garage for the cable cars. In the **Powerhouse**, you can watch how the huge gear wheels move steel cables up to 4 miles (6.5km) in length, while a collection of old cars, seats and historic photographs illustrate and explain how this old-fashioned system works. If the timing is right, you can watch how a cable is changed or a cable car repaired.

Directly in front of the museum is a stop on the Powell-Hyde Line, which runs up- and downhill as far as Russian Hill, at the corner of Hyde Street and Lombard Street, so climb aboard for a ride. It is impossible to imagine San Francisco without this unique form of transportation, which carries almost ten million passengers each year.

Grace Cathedral detail

Cable Car Barn slot machine

Powell and Market cable car

The first cable car journey took place in 1873, late at night, with the public excluded, because the authorities had no confidence in the safety of this new-fangled machine and were afraid of ridicule if it failed. They could not even find a driver, so the inventor, Andrew S. Hallidie, an English engineer, took charge of the controls.

The maiden voyage was a success and by 1894 about 100 miles (175km) of track had been laid and 500 cars were in operation. The system withstood the great earthquake well, but in 1947 city authorities decided to replace the cable cars with buses. A public campaign to keep them going proved successful. In 1964 the system was given protection as a historical monument; in 1982 $60 million was spent on restoration work. Three lines remain: California, Mason and Hyde. The cars retain the same wood and brass fittings, but the cables are no longer steam-powered, but driven electrically.

Cable cars were invented in 1873

Russian Hill probably acquired its name during the Gold Rush, when a few gravestones were discovered with inscriptions in Cyrillic script. They are thought to have marked the burial place of trappers, who originated from the Russian Fort Ross to the north of San Francisco. At the end of the 19th century, Russian Hill was a popular residential district, but most of the fine Victorian homes were destroyed during the earthquake. When land prices began to rise, the two- to three-story houses which stand here today were built.

A fine view extends from the upper end of ★ **Lombard Street** over the eastern side of the city across to Telegraph Hill. Much more famous – and often used as a backdrop for movies – is the extremely winding section of road. Until 1922, there was just a steep footpath here but, in order to accommodate the automobile, a series of zig-zag

Lombard Street views

33

bends were built into the hill. The residents later laid out gardens and planted flowers, so that in spring and summer, the hillside is smothered with a sea of blooms.

At the foot of Lombard Street and just a short distance to the north lies the **San Francisco Art Institute** ❹; a tour of this cultural landmark will interest art-lovers. Founded in 1874, it is now an important center for Bay Area art and artists. Traveling exhibitions are held in the Mediterranean-style building and sometimes it is possible to watch the students at work. The café offers a magnificent view over the city. Opening times: daily except Sunday 9am–10pm.

It is now only a few minutes' walk to **Fisherman's Wharf** (*see page 22*), where a boat trip can provide both a view back over the San Francisco skyline and a macabre but fascinating experience. From Pier 41, boats leave at regular intervals for the former prison island of ★★ **Alcatraz**. 'The Rock', as the Isla de los Alcatraces (Pelican Island) was known, became a prison after the American army fortress (1853) and military jail were abandoned. It opened in 1934 and some of America's most feared criminals – mainly those judged to be the most heinous, corrupt or beyond rehabilitation – such as Al Capone, George 'Machine Gun' Kelly and the kidnapper Alvin Karpis were incarcerated in the windowless cells. Each of the 348 cells measured 5ft (1.5m) wide, 9ft (2.75m) long and 7ft (2.13m) high and they contained a bed, a chair, a folding table, two shelves, a toilet and a small sink. Radios, TVs and newspapers were banned and only 80 percent of the inmates were allowed to receive visitors. Alcatraz prison was closed in 1963, but re-opened for tourists in 1973.

During the 39 years that the prison was in use, there were only a few attempted escapes, and all are thought to have failed. On most occasions, the escapees were caught; the rest drowned in their attempt to swim the 1½ mile (2km) channel to San Francisco.

Today, hundreds of triathletes swim the same course in about 25 minutes, while almost a million people each year sail across the Bay for a guided tour around the 12-acre (5-hectare) site, arriving at the **Sally Port**, just as the convicts did. A path then leads up to the prison building and its four cell blocks. Some cells have been restored to their original state, especially for the tourists, and they contain the blankets, the plates and cups and the personal effects that the inmates were allowed to keep. Visitors are free to walk in the prison courtyard or around the workshops, where the convicts who had earned privileges could work on their own projects. Tours daily 9.30am–5pm, every half hour. Booking recommended. Contact Blue & Gold Fleet, tel: 415/546-2700.

Alcatraz

Tourists arrive by boat

Tour 5

Mission District to the Golden Gate Bridge

Amish visitors to Golden Gate Park

Mission Dolores – Castro District – Twin Peaks – Haight-Ashbury – Golden Gate Park – Golden Gate Bridge *See map on page 36-7*

For part of this tour, which can be completed in a day, you will be following the '49 Mile Scenic Drive', a route signposted with seagull symbols that takes in all the main sights of the city. Set out by car, ideally from Market Street, and head first for the **Mission District** and the city's roots.

The Mission District takes its name from ★ **Mission Dolores** 50 on the corner of 16th Street and Dolores Street, San Francisco's oldest building and the sixth mission in a chain of Spanish settlements that stretched 600 miles (1,045km) from San Diego to northern California. Captain José Moraga and Father Francisco Palou founded the mission in 1776, just days before the signing of the Declaration of Independence by English colonists on the opposite side of the continent. In 1791 the church was dedicated to San Francisco de Assisi, and became known as Mission Dolores. It survived the 1906 earthquake almost unscathed – unlike the more modern **Mission Dolores Basilica** adjacent, which had to be rebuilt in 1918.

Once inside, look out for the statues and altars that were brought north from Mexico by donkey and also the simple ceiling paintings, which were drawn by Indians using plant dyes. In a room at the rear, a small museum contains Franciscan memorabilia. In the **cemetery** lie the last remains of the *padres* and the early settlers. Some 5,000 Ohlone Indians, who died of measles at the end of the 18th century, are buried in a mass grave nearby.

Mission Dolores stained glass

Tomb in mission cemetery

The Mission has Mexican restaurants galore

The Mission District's lively atmosphere dates from the 1960s, when thousands of immigrants from central and South America, attracted by low rents, settled here. Now, nearly all of the city's 100,000 Hispanics live in this area – almost half of them from Mexico, the rest from Cuba, El Salvador, Nicaragua and Costa Rica. The area resounds with the rhythm of salsa music. If you are feeling hungry and adventurous, drop in at one of the Mexican, Peruvian, Cuban or Puerto Rican restaurants.

Continue up palm-lined Dolores Street to **Mission Dolores Park** ❺❶, formerly a Jewish cemetery. From the southern end, a fine view extends over the city and the Spanish/Moorish buildings close by, but do not linger here after dark. The center of Mission is situated a short drive further south, around Valencia Street and Mission Street, along 24th Street and across to Alabama Street. To absorb

the sunny Latin American atmosphere, take a stroll past the shops and on to **Balmy Alley** 52, noted for its Mexican social realism-inspired murals.

Return to the car and climb up 24th Street to one of the prettiest residential areas of the city, **Noe Valley**. This is a quiet, self-contained district, almost a town on its own, with some fine Victorian houses on the hillsides.

The atmosphere heats up as soon as you turn into the **Castro District**, the most famous gay area in the US, and maybe in the world. One-of-a-kind shops, boutiques and cafés line **Castro Street**, a sort of parade ground for the ebullient residents, that stretches from the junction with Market Street as far as 19th Street. Take a look at the **Castro Theater** 53, a wonderful, decorated cinema dating from 1924. Next door is the **Names Project** 54, where

Castro Street shopping

you can buy quilts embroidered with the names of AIDS victims. Every piece remembers one person who has died of AIDS, every piece is an original. The proceeds from this initiative, which was started in 1987, go towards assisting AIDS sufferers and their relatives.

On the corner of Market and Castro Street, **Harvey Milk Plaza** 55 recalls a martyr of the gay liberation movement. Milk was the first outwardly homosexual city supervisor in San Francisco, but in 1978, together with the pro-gay mayor, George Moscone, he was shot dead by Dan White, a former supervisor. White was sentenced to only seven years for his crime, unleashing a storm of protest from the gay community. The Gay Freedom Day Parade takes places on the last Sunday in June and follows Market Street as far as the Civic Center, where the assassination took place.

Castro Street gay bar

Twin Peaks bar

Continue along 17th Street and Twin Peaks Boulevard to the highest viewpoint in the city, ★ **Twin Peaks**. Originally, these 918ft (280m) high hills were called Los Pechos de la Cola, the 'Breasts of the Young Indian Girl'. When the summer mists move in across the city, the view from up here is simply magnificent.

But the stiff breeze off the Pacific might soon send you scurrying downhill back along Twin Peaks Boulevard and then Ashbury Street into ★ **Haight-Ashbury**. Over 30 years ago, during the 1967 Summer of Love, this district around the junction of Haight Street and Ashbury Street became a magnet for America's youth. This was where the hippy movement was born, where Janis Joplin and the Grateful Dead performed and where batik shawls, sandals and flowers became symbols for a young generation in revolt, decrying the anonymity of modern society. Now, the Victorian houses once occupied by hippies

Haight-Ashbury

have been restored, many now owned by yuppies. In the streets lurk too many homeless kids and drug addicts, young people with no prospects and no ambition, quite different from the idealists of the 1960s who tried to change the world with flowers and love.

Nevertheless, it is still possible to find some relics of the hippy era. One of the shops along Haight Street, **Pipe Dreams** (1792 Haight Street) for example, still sells flower-children's paraphernalia, such as batik shirts, loose clothes, sandals, patchouli oil and hashish pipes. **Tilt!** (1433 Haight Street) has nostalgic photos that now feature on postcards or posters: trance-like figures dancing in Golden Gate Park, long-haired young men in brightly painted minibuses and 'Pearl', as Janis Joplin, the gifted singer who became the musical inspiration for the movement, was called. Her records are still very much in demand and you will find them in second-hand shops, such as **Recycled Records** (1377 Haight Street) and **Reckless Records** next door.

Janis lived round the corner in a commune at 112 Lyon Street, but there is nothing to indicate that the hippy heroine once occupied this Victorian house. A few yards further on begins the **Panhandle 56**, a long, narrow strip of green that forms the entrance to Golden Gate Park. It was here that the open-air concerts were held, where free food was distributed and where hundreds of thousands of young people in 1967 experienced the Summer of Love. On the corner of Clayton Street and Haight Street stands the **Haight-Ashbury Free Clinic 57**, initially opened to provide young people with free medical assistance, but now helping those who are HIV-positive. The history of this house mirrors the changes in society.

John F. Kennedy Drive starts at the point where the Panhandle joins Golden Gate Park and then runs on into the heart of the largest and finest of all San Francisco's open spaces. If you wish, you can rent a bicycle, roller-skates or roller-blades from one of the rental shops as an alternative to walking.

The 1,000-acre (410-hectare) and 2-mile (5-km) long **★★ Golden Gate Park** was laid out in the mid-19th century, when gold and silver from the Sierra Nevada was bringing prosperity to San Francisco. Perhaps the most important influence on its development was John McLaren, a Scotsman, who made many alterations to the design in the years between 1887 and 1943, when he was in charge. He gave the present site its character by planting thousands of trees and ornamental shrubs, he sowed flowers, dug out lakes and laid paths. He even managed to reduce the strength of the constant offshore breezes by creating a series of mounds and dips.

They call it mellow yellow

39

Free medicine for all

Golden Gate Park Buddha

Golden Gate Park sphinx

De Young Memorial Museum

Over the years, Golden Gate Park became the most popular recreational area in the city. Every weekend there was something to entertain the picnickers – from car-racing to exhibitions to open-air concerts. On Sundays, the roads are now closed to traffic and the park given over entirely to skaters, cyclists and walkers.

If you follow **John F. Kennedy Drive**, you will pass most of the park's attractions. Just past the entrance on the right-hand side stands the **Conservatory of Flowers** ❺❽, a beautiful, snow-white greenhouse in the same Victorian style as the one in London's Kew Gardens. It was commissioned in Ireland during 1875 by a millionaire by the name of James Lick, but he died a year later, so a consortium of citizens provided the finance for it to be shipped to California and then presented it to city of San Francisco. Diagonally opposite, on the south side of the road, is a modest statue of John McLaren.

A little further on along John F. Kennedy Drive, a road branches off to the left to the **Music Concourse**, an esplanade built in 1894 on the occasion of the international Midwinter Fair. On Sundays, concerts are held in the pavilion at the top end.

Several large museums are grouped nearby, including the **California Academy of Sciences** ❺❾, a natural history museum (1910) with a large planetarium. An African savannah with life-sized animals has been recreated in the **African Hall**, and skeletons and realistic models illustrate the era of the dinosaurs. The **Steinhart Aquarium** boasts more than 14,000 sea creatures.

Another facility that was built for the Midwinter Fair was the **De Young Memorial Museum** ❻⓿. Resembling an ancient Egyptian mausoleum, it was founded by the publisher M.H. de Young, who sponsored it until his death in 1925. Works by North American masters hang in the galleries, but there are also pieces from Africa, Oceania and Europe. Important traveling exhibitions are often based here and other sections are devoted to American landscape painting and the decorative arts.

Art-lovers will almost certainly want to tour the west wing of the museum, where the **Asian Art Museum** houses the famous Avery Brundage Collection. Brundage was, for many years, the president of the International Olympic Committee. This is the biggest museum of its kind outside Asia, but it does not have the space to exhibit everything it owns (the museum plans to move to new premises within the next decade, *see page 24*). At any one time, only 15 percent of the entire collection is on show. However, the exhibitions are frequently changed.

After a tiring tour of the galleries, sit down in the **Japanese Tea Garden** ❻ and enjoy a refreshing cup of tea. The gardens here are a mini-labyrinth of pagodas, ornate bridges, ponds and pavilions. When the cherry trees are in blossom in April, the whole garden has a fairy-tale quality. The main attraction is the **Amazarashi-no-ho-take-Buddha** or the 'seated Buddha who does not shelter from the rain or sun'. This 10ft (3m) high bronze figure was cast in Japan in 1770. It was in the tea house here in 1909 that the Japanese gardener, Makota Hagiwara, invented the famous fortune cookie. The idea was later copied by restaurants in Chinatown but many people from San Francisco to Hong Kong labor under the illusion that the cookies are an old Chinese tradition.

If you have time to spare, then take the opportunity to cycle round **Stow Lake** or explore it by boat. The biggest of the 11 lakes in the park, its attractions include the 413ft (126m) high **Strawberry Hill**, which the railroad magnate, Huntington, commissioned and also a **Chinese Pagoda** (1976), a present to San Francisco from the citizens of China. It was transported to the West Coast in 6,000 separate pieces.

At the western end of the park, beside the roaring waves of the Pacific, the Great Highway runs southwards to **Fort Funston**, a former coastal fortification, but now a favorite take-off point for hang-gliders. **San Francisco Zoo** ❻, on Sloat Boulevard, is famous for its **Gorilla World** and its breeding program for koala bears – it is worth a visit but allow plenty of time if you want to see everything.

Japanese Tea Garden

Park pagoda

Cliff House sign

Rodin's Palace sculpture

42

Golden Gate Bridge lookout

Follow the Great Highway northwards alongside the broad sandy beach of the **Golden Gate National Recreation Area** to the **Cliff House** ❻❸. The simple wooden structure that was built on this high cliff in 1863 was originally intended as a restaurant, but it was also used as a brothel. When it burned down, it was replaced with the splendid Victorian neo-classical mansion that can be seen today. Although the restaurant itself does not have very much to commend it, the ★ **Musée Mécanique** in the basement has a fine collection of games machines. A little further along Point Lobos Avenue take a detour into 45th Avenue to another building of architectural interest: the **Veterans Administration Medical Center** ❻❹, a fine Art Deco building which can only be viewed from outside.

Continue further to the pines of **Lincoln Park** for the **California Palace of the Legion of Honor** ❻❺. This arts museum is mainly known for its excellent collection of Rodin sculptures. It was built in 1924 as a replica of France's Palais de la Légion d'Honneur in memory of the Californian soldiers who died in World War I.

From El Camino del Mar and Lincoln Boulevard, the prettiest section of the 49-Mile Scenic Drive, there are spectacular views over the Golden Gate, with beautiful mansions on all sides. Almost the whole of this coastal strip belongs to the **Golden Gate National Recreation Area**, an extensive nature reserve and popular leisure area. If you want to stretch your legs, then take a walk down to **Baker Beach**.

Soon the narrow straits that form the entrance to the Bay, the Golden Gate, will come into view, and with that, of course, the ★★★ **Golden Gate Bridge**, the city's most famous symbol. The full splendor of this vast, reddish-gold structure can be appreciated from a viewpoint near the access road on the south side of the bridge. A bronze memorial of Joseph B. Strauss, the man who built the bridge, looks down on the throngs of visitors. You can cross the bridge on foot or else take the car (a toll is payable for the return journey). The **Vista Point** on the north side affords another panoramic view of the bridge, the city and the Bay. But the view from the winding road which climbs up to the **Marin Headlands** from the first exit at the north end of the bridge, is even better. On a mist-free day, ideally just before sunset, the full splendor of the city and the Golden Gate Bridge unfolds.

When the idea of a bridge was first proposed, the risks were thought to be too great. The problems of distance (1¼ miles/2km), the depth of the water (318ft/97m) and the incredibly powerful tides seemed insuperable.

Work began in 1933 and the job took four years; at the time it was thought to be a technical miracle and it has certainly stood the test of time.

The two towers in Art Deco style reach a height of 746ft (227m) above sea-level and when they were built, they were the highest structures in the country outside New York. The deck, some 250ft (75m) above the water, is held in place by immensely strong cables nearly 1½ miles (2.3km) long and 3ft (90cm) thick. It cost $35 million and, with a span of 3,950ft (1,280m) was, at the time, the longest suspension bridge in the world. The bridge was opened in May, 1937. During the Great Depression the project, which had received money from federal job creation funds, kept many people in work.

Now some 50 million vehicles every year use the six-lane roadway – the original plans were for only 4 million – and so, with serious traffic jams, calls for a second crossing have been increasing. Plans for a second roadway underneath, possibly with a rail track as well, have also been discussed. Whatever happens, the Golden Gate Bridge will continue to be a fitting symbol for the city.

On the south side of the bridge, take the first exit on the right and, after passing under Highway 101, take Marine Drive down to **Fort Point** ❻❻, a fortress built between 1853 and 1861 to secure the entrance to the Bay. Of the 126 cannons that were installed here, none was ever fired in anger, but this surf-sprayed spot offers a dramatic perspective on the vast bridge.

Lincoln Boulevard now winds gently through the old military **Presidio** site back to the city center. The Spanish set up the first outpost here and during World War II the complex became the headquarters for the 6th Army – as the huge barracks and military cemetery testify. A few years ago the army decided to vacate the area, but the site was granted protected status and will probably be turned into parkland.

Bridge with a view

Military cemetery, Presidio

Fort Point

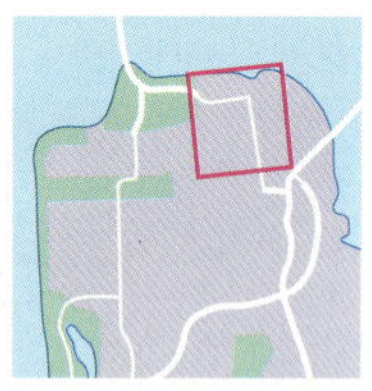

Tour 6

Off the Beaten Track

Fort Mason – Marina District – Palace of Fine Arts – Union Street – Pacific Heights – Fillmore Street – Japantown – Alamo Square *See map on pages 36–7*

Fort Mason

This is a tour for visitors who have time to explore off the beaten track. You may like to rent a car, but it can be done on foot with one or two taxi rides for the longer hops. In any event, the entire tour will take under a day.

It is not far from Fisherman's Wharf or the cable car terminus by Hyde Street to this tour's starting point, the former military base of **Fort Mason** ❻❼. Before the land around it was reclaimed from the sea, the fort stood on a peninsula which jutted deep into the Bay and where the Spanish built their first fortifications before 1800. During World War II, US operations in the Pacific were directed from here, and it was also the command center for the military during the Korean War.

In 1962 the fortress was finally abandoned and the long huts were put to a peaceful use. Now, around 50 charitable and alternative lifestyle organizations occupy the site, which has plenty of space for museums, theaters, art galleries and workshops, even the vegetarian Buddhist restaurant, **Green's** *(see page 60)*. Among the most interesting sights are the **Mexican Museum of San Francisco** (Building D) and the **Museo Italo Americano** (Building C), which focus on the history and art of two of the city's largest immigrant groups.

Marina District boats

The **Golden Gate Promenade** runs westward along the coast to the foot of the Golden Gate Bridge some 3 miles (5km) further on – a pleasant walk for a sunny day. **Marina Green** ❻❽ is situated at the start of the promenade. The park forms part of the popular **Marina District**, an area that did not exist before the 1920s. After the 1906 earthquake, rubble and debris were deposited in the sea to create new land. Renovated after the 1989 earthquake, which caused considerable damage, the pastel shades of the houses give the district a slightly Mediterranean feel.

Palace of Fine Arts

At the eastern end of the Marina District stands the last remnant of the **Panama Pacific Exposition** of 1915, the ★ **Palace of Fine Arts** ❻❾. Designed by the architect Bernhard Maybeck in Greek and Italian architectural styles, the building was made from plaster, as it was only intended to last for the duration of the exhibition. In 1962, however, it was decided to reconstruct the circular structure with its delightful colonnade. Since 1969, the pavilion at the north end of the rotunda has housed one of the

city's most varied museums, the ★ **Exploratorium**, founded by Frank Oppenheimer, brother of the inventor of the atom bomb. Various experiments enable the young and the curious to feel, smell, see, hear and taste modern technology, chemistry and physics.

Carry on through the Marina District along **Chestnut Street**, a popular thoroughfare which, to the east of Divisadero Street, is lined with fashion shops, restaurants and coffee houses. In **Cow Hollow** a little further on and running parallel to Chestnut Street is **Union Street**, still one of the best shopping streets in the city. Of architectural interest is the **Vedanta Temple** ⑦ on the corner of Filbert Street and Webster Street. This wooden house was built in 1905 by the Hindu Vedanta Society in a blend of Victorian and Moorish styles. The unusual **Octagon House** ⑦ on the corner of Union Street and Gough Street dates from 1861.

You can climb up into the upscale residential district of ★ **Pacific Heights** via Gough Street or one of the other streets that run parallel. Right from the early days, this was an area for the wealthy, who could afford to experiment with different architectural styles: a miscellany of Victorian, Baroque and Colonial was possible, in fact, anything went, as long as it was attractive and extravagant. The finest houses stand on the hill around ★ **Lafayette Park** and ★ **Alta Plaza Park** four streets further east. Both of these open spaces afford magnificent views over the city. The Victorian **Haas-Lilienthal House** ⑦ (2007 Franklin Street), the exclusive **Spreckels Mansion** ⑦ (2000 Washington Street) and **Schubert Hall** ⑦ (2099 Pacific Avenue) are the pick of the bunch.

Further south, at the heart of **Japantown**, is the **Japan Center** ⑦, a combination of cultural center and shopping mall. It extends for about three blocks around the peace pagoda – a gift from Japan – between Post Street and Geary Boulevard. Various Japanese shops, some good restaurants and tea-houses are to be found in the complex. The **Nihonmachi Mall** in Buchanan Street, designed to resemble a Japanese village, is more stylish.

Before returning to the center, head for ★ **Alamo Square**, one of the prettiest squares in San Francisco and one which offers a much-photographed view of the skyline. As this is not one of the safest parts of the city, it's best to go by taxi or car. The square is surrounded by a fine collection of 'Painted Ladies', as the magnificent Victorian houses are called. The graceful beauties are classed as 'Queen Anne Style', which dates from the end of the 19th century and is characterized by pointed gables, tiny oriel windows and rounded archways. To stand and admire the pastel shades of **Steiner Street**, set against the stunning city skyline, is a fitting way to end this tour.

Exploratorium adventure

Union Street

Alamo Square

Eureka
Healdsburg
Calistoga
Angwin
Portland
Woodland
Lake Berryessa
505
Davis
80
Guerneville
Bothe-Napa Valley S. P.
St. Helena
Winters
Sacramento
3
128
Rutherford
Santa Rosa
Dixon
101
Yountville
Clarksburg
Bodega
Glen Ellen
29
121
Vacaville
5
1
12
Sonoma
Napa
Petaluma
3
3
12
Fairfield
12
Rio Vista
Walnut Grove
Inverness
37
80
680
Vallejo
Sacramento River
160
Pt. Reyes Light Station
101
780
San Pablo Bay
Pt. Reyes National Seashore
Novato
Antioch
Concord
3
580
San Pablo
Brentwood
Richmond
Walnut Creek
Clayton
Muir Woods N. M.
1
Berkeley
Mt. Diablo 1174
Mt. Diablo S. P.
Sausalito
4
80
2
Oakland
San Francisco
Alameda
San Leandro
580
46
South San Francisco
4
580
Livermore
580
Farallon Islands
San Francisco Bay
Hayward
Pacifica
880
101
San Mateo
Redwood City
Fremont
San Carlos
Palo Alto
680
1
280
4
Mtn. View
San Gregorio
Sunnyvale
84
Santa Clara
San Jose
35
Mt. Hamilton 1283
9
17
PACIFIC
Saratoga
Big Basin Redwoods S. P.
Los Gatos
Henry W. Coe State Park
236
OCEAN
9
Boulder Creek
Morgan Hill
Felton
101
Davenport
Soquel
152
Gilroy
Henry Cowell Redwoods S. P.
Santa Cruz
Capitola
4
Watsonville
Monterey
1
Hollister
156
Bay
Castroville
N
Fremont Peak S. P.
Marina
Salinas
Pacific Grove
1
EXCURSIONS
4
Monterey
68
Salinas R.
101
0   20 miles
Carmel
0   20 km
Pt. Lobos State Res.
Gonzales
Big Sur
Los Angeles
Reno
Los Angeles
DIABLO RANGE

Excursion 1

Sausalito and Muir Woods *See map on page 46*

The wind-swept, mist-soaked towns of Marin County, just a ferry ride away from San Francisco, have long attracted city-dwellers. You can dine in old-fashioned, uncrowded restaurants and sleep in pretty bed and breakfast inns, sift for sand dollars on lonely beaches or hike on mossy wilderness paths. The closest of these towns to San Francisco is ★ **Sausalito**, a former fishing village just a short hop away on the Market Street ferry. Commuters use this boat, and it's not uncommon for friendships to be forged or business contacts to be exchanged on the churning, rolling journey to and from town. But do note that the ferry, and the town, can become crowded on weekends.

The name Sausalito is a corruption of the Spanish word *saucelito*, meaning "little willow". The town's waterside ambience, the warrens of (expensive) boutiques and its pretty houses perched behind them on a steep slope down to the Bay draw ineviable comparisons to Mediterranean villages. Its main street is the **Bridgeway**, which ambles in a good-natured fashion past shops likely to appeal to tourists with money in their pockets. The town has not always had such a well-heeled image, however. When it was an important shipping link between Northern California and San Francisco, this same street was full of innumerable saloons, brothels and gambling houses. It also served as a base for liquor bootleggers who supplied the speakeasies of San Francisco.

Not far away is ★ **Muir Woods National Monument,** a small grove about 12 miles (20km) north of San Francisco and easy to reach via Highway 101 and Highway 1. Some magnificent redwoods – the tallest trees in the world – have survived in this reserve, situated in a narrow valley of the coast mountains. About 140 million years ago, huge forests of redwood trees *(sequoia sempervirens)* covered large areas of the northern hemisphere but, in more recent times, these giants, which can grow to 360ft (110m) and live for 2,500 years, have only survived along the north coast of California. In 1908, the last section of original woodland was declared a national monument by President Roosevelt.

The woods were named after the naturalist, John Muir, the founding father of the American conservation movement. A small exhibition in the **Visitor Center** details the life story of these prehistoric giants. Afterwards, follow the 6-mile (10km) trails along **Redwood Creek** where the trees grow to 260ft (80m). One of the footpaths leads up the slopes of 2,600ft (800m) **Mount Tamalpais**,with its fine views over the whole of the San Francisco Bay.

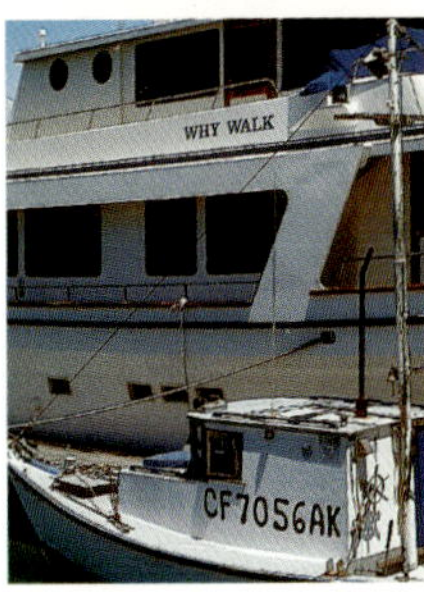

Sausalito marina and waterfront

47

Redwoods can live for 2500 years

View from Mount Tamalpais

Writer Jack London lived here

Excursion 2

Oakland and Berkeley *See map on page 46*

Oakland Harbor

For over 150 years, **Oakland** has had to play second string to its better-known neighbor on the other side of the 8-mile (13km) long San Francisco – **Oakland Bay Bridge**, but this harbor and business center has a certain appeal in its own right. Tucked into the hillside communities behind Oakland are some of the Bay Area's most expensive homes, many now rebuilt following the fires earlier this decade that swept through the Oakland hills, destroying over 3,000 structures and killing 25 people. Cheapter rents and a slightly slower urban place have attracted would-be San Franciscans to this town that has its own Chinatown and thriving waterfront area, but with fewer crowds.

Oakland's version of Fisherman's Wharf is the pedestrian **Jack London Square**, where the famous writer grew up. The **First and Last Chance Saloon** which London frequented is here, as is his sod-roofed Yukon cabin, bodily dismantled and shipped from Alaska. On Sundays, there's a **farmers' market**, open until early afternoon.

Oakland's most obvious landmarks are the distinctive ower of the **Tribune Building**; **City Hall**, with its wedding cake copola; and, in the hills above the city, the five-owered, white granite **Mormon Temple**. Also visible rom the Nimitz Freeway, if you're driving toward the airport, is the Oakland-Alameda County **Coliseum** complex, home of the Oakland A's baseball team, and the Golden State Warriors basketball team.

The **Oakland Museum** (1000 Oak Street), has a large exhibition illustrating the history, natural history and geology of California. The **African American Museum** s at 5606 San Pablo Avenue (from summer 1997: 659

Oakland exhibit

14th Street). For many blacks, Oakland has a special significance. It was here during the 1960s that the Black Panther Movement, the militant civil rights movement, was founded. The Black Panthers enjoyed a very high profile during this most turbulent of decades.

Berkeley is the home of the ★ **University of California**. Founded in 1873, several Nobel prize winners have taught at this educational hothouse, and, like Oakland, the university has a radical tradition. It was the Free Speech Movement of 1964 that first put Berkeley on the map. At issue was an administration order limiting political activities on campus. This touched off massive student protests and, in turn, similar protests on campuses throughout America. For several years thereafter, Berkeley was a smoldering center of protest and politics.

In 1969, students once more took to the streets to stop the university's expansion into an area they wanted to preserve as **People's Park**. They ultimately prevailed, despite the intervention of 2,000 National Guard troops and violence that led to the death of an onlooker. Today, apart from a few stands selling political literature, few signs of strident movements are visible among the cafés and bookshops along **Telegraph Avenue**, but this is still the place to buy jewelry, pottery, and tie-dyed everything.

Berkeley campus

On the approach to Berkeley, two buildings stand out. One is a fairy-tale white palace on a hillside towards the south – the **Claremont Resort Hotel**, which, like San Francisco's Palace of Fine Arts, was finished just before the Panama Pacific Exposition of 1915. The other landmark is a tall, thin, pointed structure, the university's bell tower. Its official name is **Sather Tower**, but it is known to all simply as **The Campanile**, because it was modeled after St Mark's Campanile in Venice, Italy. The 308ft (94m) high tower was built in 1914 and affords a fine view of Berkeley, the Bay, San Francisco and the Golden Gate Bridge. It's worth the climb to the top.

The Campanile

Up **Strawberry Canyon** is the university's **Botanical Gardens**, a sweet-smelling place filled with over 25,000 species of South American, South African, European and Australian plants. Further along **Centennial Drive** is the university's **Lawrence Science Hall**, where weekend visitors conduct biology experiments or operate computer terminals.

Downtown Berkeley

At the 'top of the world' (or at least the campus) is **Tilden Park**. A leisurely place to picnic or hike here is along **Lake Anza**. Other attractions include the **steam trains** which pass through fields and eucalyptus groves. There are also a few small museums on the university grounds, such as the **Museum of Anthropology** in Kroeber Hall. The **Student Union** (tel: 510/642-5215) can organize tours of many of the sights on campus.

Sonoma and Napa Valleys *See map on page 46*

Numerous wineries in these regions are open to the public, the restaurants provide fine California cuisine and the delightful valleys and vineyards are a feast for the eyes. It is possible to cover this whole area in one day (110 miles/180km) from San Francisco or a tour could be broken down into a two- or three-day excursion. Finding somewhere to stay 'on spec' in spring, the height of summer, or during the wine harvest in the fall is not always easy, however.

About an hour's drive (45 miles/70km) to the north of San Francisco on Highway 12 lies ★ **Sonoma Valley** with its principal town, **Sonoma**. This pretty town was an important center during the Spanish era. On June 14, 1846, the first flag of the California Republic was hoisted on its central plaza, and memories of these days survive in the old buildings of **Sonoma State Historic Park**. Modern Sonoma's role as the center of its vine-growing region dates from around this time, too. Missionaries planted the first vines here, in order to produce wine for religious services. Two men in particular – Father Jose Altimira, the founder of the Mission San Francisco de Solano at Sonoma, and General Vallejo, who colonized Sonoma and Napa counties with land grants to his relatives and friends – dabbled in early California winemaking. (Two blocks from Sonoma Plaza stand the **Sabastiani Vineyards**, some of which can be traced to the mission days.) But it was Count Agoston Haraszthy who pushed the Sonoma region into wine stardom.

Haraszthy, a flamboyant Hungarian political refugee, began **Buena Vista** in 1857 (Old Winery Road, on the outskirts of Sonoma), making Buena Vista the oldest winery in California. He treked across Europe to cull wine-grape cuttings for local growers. One of Haraszthy's proteges, Charles Krug, discovered that the climate and soil in the long valleys north of San Francisco were ideal for several types of viticulture, and in 1861 opened the Napa Valley's first commerical winery. By the 1880s, the wines were winning medals in Europe.

Prohibition at the start of this century set the industry back but, during the 1930s, new vines were planted. Forty years later, wine production reached new commercial heights, with Cabernet Sauvignon, Merlot, Chardonnay, Zinfandel and Pinot Blanc the main grape varieties. By the 1990s, there were over 200 vine-growers.

Follow the narrow country road northwards from near **Glen Ellen**, along the hairpin turns of the Oakville Grade

Barracks of historic Sonoma

Sonoma produces both wine and cheese

over the mountains. After about 25 miles (40km), the ★ **Napa Valley** begins, running parallel to Sonoma. Wineries line Highway 29, the main route through the 30-mile (50km) long valley, from the town of **Napa** in the south as far as the attractive, historic town of **Calistoga** in the north. Despite the huge numbers of visitors, Napa Valley retains a surprisingly tranquil atmosphere, and picnic spots are numerous.

In the towns of **Yountville**, **Rutherford** and **St Helena**, it's possible to find both wine tasting centers and good restaurants serving California cuisine. Calistoga is famous for its hot springs and bottled mineral water, its mud baths popular with the 'beautiful people' of northern California as a unique form of beauty treatment.

The guided tours in the California mission-style **Winery Robert Mondavi** in Rutherford (7801 St Helena Highway, Oakville) will shed light on the high-tech processes used in modern wine production. The **Domaine Chandon Winery** (One California Drive, Yountville) is French both in technology and in style. The winery, owned by Chandon (of Moët fame), makes sparkling wine in the *methode champenoise* fashion; that is, it is fermented in the same bottle from which it is poured. The winery's elegant indoor/outdoor restaurant serves classic French food.

There are at least 80 other wineries in Napa Valley. A selective list would include the **Clos Pegase** (1060 Dunaweal Lane, Calistoga), built by the top architect Michael Graves after winning a major architectural design competition for his earth and russet-colored dwelling, and the **Sterling Winery**, with its clean modern architectural lines and magnificent views over the valley (by Highway 29, just before Calistoga).

The route back to San Francisco on I-80 is a fast and straightforward one.

Valley vineyards

Wine by the barrel

51

Fertile fields of grapes

Capitola

Excursion 4

Silicon Valley and the Monterey Peninsula
See map on page 46

The Monterey Peninsula lies about 150 miles (250km) south of San Francisco. Despite the distance, this spot is a popular haunt for those escaping the city. Allow two to three days for this excursion and, if possible, avoid weekends as hotels will almost certainly be full.

Take Highway 101 along the west coast of the Bay to Santa Clara, or **Silicon Valley**. The famous research institute founded in 1891, **Stanford University**, is here, as well as world-famous names such as Apple and Hewlett Packard. In the scores of smaller companies located in the valley, computer wizards are writing tomorrow's software.

In **San Jose**, the region's main town, the **Tech Museum of Innovation** (145 West San Carlos Street) documents the history of Silicon Valley and the computer industry. At the north end of the town is an attraction of a very different kind: the **Winchester Mystery House**, a villa with 160 rooms, 10,000 windows and 2,000 doors. Sarah Winchester, who built this bizarre house, was the millionaire heiress of the famous armaments manufacturer.

She thought she was being persecuted by the spirits of those who had died from bullets fired from Winchester rifles and believed that these spirits could only be scared off by the sound of constant hammering. So, for 38 years until her death in 1922, workmen hammered away on her home, building a virtual labyrinth of rooms. The adjoining museum exhibits the Winchester's arms collection (525 S. Winchester Boulevard).

Highway 9 and SR236 climb out of San Jose and over the coastal mountain ridge. High up in the hills, in ★ **Big Basin Redwoods State Park**, stand the last great redwood trees south of San Francisco. If you would prefer to avoid the narrow, winding SR236, you can stay on Highway 9 and then take a half-hour stroll past the redwoods in **Henry Cowell State Park**, a little further to the west.

The college town of **Santa Cruz** and then **Capitola**, a typical beach resort, are not far away. Then, pick up Highway 1 to follow the curves of broad Monterey Bay. During the spring, the high sand-dunes by the coast are covered in a colorful carpet of marigolds. After a little while, the ★ **Monterey Peninsula** begins. For many Californians, this is one of the prettiest sections of the Pacific Coast, with its cypress woods and battered cliffs.

The busy city (pop. 300,000) of **Monterey** lies at the north end of the 7-mile (10km) long peninsula. For most visitors the magnet is **Fisherman's Wharf**. The **Path of**

Monterey's Cannery Row

Dolphin sculpture, Monterey

52

History, a 2-mile (3km) long signposted trail, starts opposite the pier by the renovated **Custom House** (1827). The main points of interest along the route are Mexican houses made from adobe bricks, the first theater and the old hotel where the writer of *Treasure Island* lived in 1879. **Stevenson House**, like the other adobe houses, has been restored, furnished in the style of the day and is now a museum (530 Houston Street).

Monterey's wharf

Another writer is also associated with Monterey: John Steinbeck, author of *Cannery Row* (1938). The harbor area (**Cannery Row**), lies just to the west of the old town. For many years it was the center of the sardine fishing industry, but now its old factories have been converted into hotels, restaurants and shops. ★ **Monterey Bay Aquarium** is the main attraction by the wharf. The prized exhibit is the 30ft (10m) high tank of kelp forest, but it also fascinating to watch the sea otters crushing mussels. Try to be around at feeding time, when staff don wetsuits and microphones to talk to the audience while underwater (886 Cannery Row; daily 9am–6pm).

Probably the prettiest section of the peninsula is the **17-Mile Drive** (toll payable), a panoramic route that runs beside the cliffs passing golf courses, rocky bays and beautiful homes. **Carmel** lies at the end of the drive. This town with oddly-shaped stone houses and a magnificent white beach was founded shortly after 1900 by artists from San Francisco, and the overgrown streets have retained some of this charm. On the southern outskirts of town, the **San Carlos Borromeo mission** was founded in 1771 by Father Junipero Serra. The stone church and tower dome have been beautifully restored (3080 Rio Road) and the gardens are particularly attractive.

Carmel's mission and beach

A few miles further south by Highway 1 lies ★ **Point Lobos State Reserve**, a section of coastline with colonies of sea lions and pretty picnic spots by the roaring ocean.

ONE WAY

Art and Architecture

Opposite: painting the city's 'Painted Ladies'

Architecture

The urban landscape of San Francisco is dominated by the **Victorian style**. Books about the city always show picturesque rows of houses with ornate woodwork, oriel windows and carved facades. Some 14,000 of these 'Painted Ladies' from the late 19th century have survived earthquakes and renovation programs. They were usually built by the wealthy middle classes, who favored such districts as Pacific Heights, Noe Valley and Haight-Ashbury. The best-known example of **Queen Anne style**, which came in around 1890, are the houses in Steiner Street, by Alamo Square (*see Tour 6, page 45*).

The **Spanish style** of contructing houses with adobe bricks was once much in evidence, but, apart from one or two notable exceptions, such as the Dolores Mission (*see Tour 5, page 35*), they have not stood the test of time.

Spanish-style Mission Dolores

The fashion for Victorian architecture lasted from 1860 to 1900, but, after the 1906 earthquake, the **classical style** became the vogue, exemplified by the Civic Center (*see Tour 2, page 24*) and some of the first multi-story blocks in the Financial District.

During the 1930s and with the support of federal government money, several mammoth projects were initiated, the most important being the Golden Gate Bridge (*see Tour 5, page 42*) and the Oakland Bay Bridge (*see Excursion 2, page 48*). Both are impressive pieces of civil engineering in the **Art Deco style**.

Classic City Hall

During the 1920s when New York and Chicago were building ever higher skyscrapers than San Francisco, the architects by the Bay still dreaded the consequences of the area's most horrific natural disorder – earthquakes. For the first half of this century, few buildings exceeded 15 floors. During the 1960s, however, the upper limit of modern architecture was raised, and then, during the 1970s, special techniques for making tall buildings safe from earthquakes evolved, allowing for the construction of such signature buildings as the Financial District's Transamerica Pyramid (*see Tour 3, page 29*) which commands attention because of its size and shape.

All new skyscrapers in this **modern style** have a flexible steel corset. Movement is allowed for in the specifications but it is restrained by 'shock absorbers'. Just a few feet below the Financial District lies solid bedrock, which is relatively unaffected by earthquakes. The 1989 quake, which registered 7.1 on the Richter scale, put these new methods to the test: the 50-story blocks in the Financial District were hardly damaged. It was the Marina District, where three- to four-story houses are built on loose, reclaimed land, that suffered the most.

Since the 1980s, numerous post-modern tower blocks have risen up in the Financial District. At the same time, the city's grand Victorian residential areas, such as Noe Valley, have been restored to their former glory.

San Francisco's murals

The art of mural painting arrived in San Francisco at the beginning of the 20th century. Diego Riviera, one of the first practitioners, brought the art form from Mexico where *social realismo* was very popular. The boom years for murals were the 1960s, especially in the predominantly Mexican neighborhood of the **Mission District**. There are over 500 paintings in this area alone – look in Balmy Alley and the area around the junction of 24th Street and Mission Street (*see Tour 5, page 37*).

Themes include the day-to-day lives of the Latino settlers, pre-Columbian myths and futuristic visions. In 1977, a club was formed to support mural artists, to organize exhibitions, to run workshops and to arrange walks through the Mission District for artists to show and explain their works. The tours, which last about two hours, start outside the office of the Precita Eyes Murals Arts Center, 348 Precita Avenue/Folsom Street, tel: 415/285-2287. The tours take place on Saturdays at 1.30pm

Literature

San Francisco has been a popular destination for writers ever since the last century. **Mark Twain** visited the city during the Gold Rush and **Robert Louis Stevenson**, the author of *Treasure Island*, stayed in the Bay Area some 30 years later. But the region also produced its own literary figures: **John Steinbeck** (*Grapes of Wrath* and *Cannery Row)* was born in Salinas, California; **Jack London** grew up in Oakland; and the dramatist **William Saroyan** lived in San Francisco in 1920 and again after World War II. The celebrated crime writer **Dashiell Hammett** spent his most productive years (1921–9) in the Bay Area. His world-weary detective Sam Spade, the hero of the best-selling *The Maltese Falcon* (1930), spent much of his time scouring the city's streets in search of clues.

The 1950s were probably the city's most lively literary years. The young, rebellious poets of the Beat Generation moved from New York, led a Bohemian lifestyle in and around North Beach and – through their writings and their behavior – sought to pillory the *petit bourgeois* conventions of Middle America. **Allen Ginsberg** wrote his poem *Howl* in 1955 while living in San Francisco and in 1957 **Jack Kerouac** published *On the Road*, an important influence on the 1960s youth movement and a source of inspiration for the innovative **Ken Kesey** (*One Flew Over the Cuckoo's Nest*; 1963).

Mural magic, Haight-Ashbury

Market Street mural

Jack London

Events Calendar

February Chinese New Year celebrations last for two weeks. The highlight is the colorful dragon parade along Market Street to Columbus Avenue.

March 17 St Patrick's Day is the day when the Irish community and fiddlers parade along Market Street.

Mid-April When the cherry trees are in bloom in Golden Gate Park, the Japanese celebrate Cherry Blossom Festival with tea ceremonies, drum concerts and a parade from City Hall to Japantown.

May 5 Latin-American immigrants in the Mission District celebrate the Mexican Revolution with food, fiestas and parades.

Mid-June North Beach Festival – San Francisco's oldest street fair with live bands and street stalls.

End of June The Lesbian Gay Freedom Parade along Market Street is held on the last Sunday of the month. Not just about gay rights, it's also a memorial march for the city's AIDS victims.

July 4 Independence Day celebrations with a fireworks display on the Crissy Field in the Presidio.

Beginning of July Jazz & All That Art music festival with bands and street theater in Fillmore Street.

Beginning of August Nihonmachi Street Fair takes place in Japantown.

September Shakespeare's plays performed throughout the month in Golden Gate Park.

End of September The San Francisco Blues Festival in Fort Mason and at the Embarcadero Center attracts some of America's best blues singers.

Beginning of October The Castro Street Fair is another opportunity for gays to join forces and express themselves.

Mid-October San Francisco Jazz Festival, two weeks of top bands from all over the country playing at various venues around town.

December Union Square and North Beach are the main meeting places for New Year's Eve celebrations.

Dragons, February

Live music at the North Beach Festival, June

57

Gays take pride in the Castro Street Fair, October

Food and Drink

Opposite: fresh off the boat

With over 3,000 eating and drinking establishments – more per capita than anywhere else in the world – and its rich ethnic diversity, San Francisco is one of the world's great culinary capitals. When you wander down the street you can't help but take in each neighborhood's fascination with food. Each area of the city features authentic restaurants that cater to discriminating locals and travelers. It was always like this: San Francisco once boasted the only restaurant in America serving pizza. The country's first Northern Chinese restaurant opened here. Irish Coffee and other food and beverage delights were invented in the saloons and cafés of San Francisco.

One of the reasons why eating out in San Francisco is such a pleasure is because the city's chefs have ideal ingredients from which to choose. Almost every kind of fruit and vegetable grows in California's Central Valley, the most fertile agricultural region in the US. Citrus fruit comes from southern California, milk, cheese, lamb and beef from northern California. The nearby fertile valleys produce wonderful wines, while the Pacific Ocean provides plentiful fresh fish. Many of these ingredients are combined in dishes which go under the banner heading **California Cuisine**: fresh produce, but often served with exotic sauces, like salmon with Thai curry, or Californian partridge with Caribbean spices and Mexican salsa. Many of the seafood restaurants around Fisherman's Wharf serve **clam chowder**, served with San Francisco's traditional, slightly bitter-tasting **sourdough bread**.

Today, the pizza ovens in the Italian eateries of **North Beach** are rivals to those in Rome or Naples. These are in addition to the slightly shabby *trattoria* or little cafés where old men sip espresso and gossip. Only a few minutes' walk from North Beach is **Chinatown** where roast duck, goose, rabbit and sausages hang in many of the windows. **Dim sum** restaurants have become very popular in recent years. *Dim sum*, meaning 'little hearts', are delicate meat, fish or vegetable pastries that the waiter or waitress brings round on trolleys. You point to what you want and the bill is calculated according to the number of empty bowls left on the table. The choice is not limited to Chinese and Italian food, however. The city boasts countless Japanese restaurants serving **sushi**, delicacies that contain fresh fish from the Pacific. You can also expect to find Greek, Indian, Spanish, French, Creole, and German restaurants, all serving native dishes. In Haight-Ashbury, the Fillmore District and along Union Street, Mexican restaurants have become particularly popular.

Casual dress is perfectly acceptable for lunch or dinner in most restuarants. It is often advisable, however, to

Farmers' Market favorite

59

Steak or seafood for lunch?

Chowder in sourdough bread

Chef's specialties

Ladies who lunch

book a table in advance, and dinner is usually served between 7 and 10pm. Preferred drink is either beer or one of the excellent wines from the Napa or Sonoma valleys. (*see pages 50 and 51*).

Restaurant selection

The following suggestions are listed according to three categories: $$$ = expensive (from $50); $$ = moderate ($25-50); $ = inexpensive (up to $25).

San Francisco
Bix, 56 Gold Street, tel: 433-6300. Like a 1930s New York jazz club but with uptown-style California cuisine and occasional jazz concerts to accompany dinner. $$$

Carnelian Room, 555 California Street, tel: 433-7500. Fine dining on the 52nd story of the Bank of America building. Wear a jacket and tie. Fabulous view. $$$

Fleur de Lys, 777 Sutter Street, tel: 673-7779. One of the best restaurants in the US. Top-class French cuisine in a setting created by an award-winning designer. Hubert Keller from Alsace is the chef. $$$

North Beach Restaurant, 1512 Stockton Street, tel: 392-1700. Excellent Italian cuisine, comparable with many top restaurants in Milan or Florence. Since its conversion from trattoria to ristorante, this North Beach eatie is the perfect place for a civilized evening. $$–$$$

Postrio, 545 Post Street, tel: 776-7825. If you want to be part of the San Francisco style scene, then this is the place to be seen. Wolfgang Puck, the master of California gourmet cooking, is the owner of this top restaurant in the Hotel Prescott, whose art gallery-style dining room is packed seven days a week. $$–$$$

Aqua, 252 California Street, tel: 956-9662. Modern restaurant in the heart of the Financial District with a large business clientele and low-key Italo-French cuisine. The fish dishes are highly recommended. $$

Elite Café, 2049 Fillmore Street, tel: 346-8668. A long-established fish restaurant in 'old San Francisco' style. Very attentive waiters. $$

Green's, Fort Mason, Building A, tel: 771-6222. Vegetarian cuisine prepared by Buddhist cooks, so more than just salads and muesli. Housed in an old warehouse with a fine view over the Golden Gate Bridge, Green's is especially spectacular at sunset. $$

Dim sum

Imperial Palace, 919 Grant Avenue, tel: 982-8889. Large Chinese restaurant in the heart of Chinatown. Excellent dim sum. $$

McCormick & Kuletos, 900 North Point Street, tel: 929-1730. One of the best restaurants on Fisherman's Wharf. By Ghirardelli Square, with a great view over the Bay. Recommended for steaks and seafood. $$

Miss Pearl's Jam House, 601 Eddy Street, tel: 775-5276. Spicy Caribbean food with a view of the pool and a tropical atmosphere. Live reggae from Thursday to Saturday. $$

Oritalia, 1915 Fillmore Street, tel: 346-1333. Small but elegant restaurant serving excellent California cuisine to beautiful people. Reservations essential. $$

Peppers waiting for the pot

Tadich Grill, 240 California Street, tel: 391-1849. One of San Francisco's oldest restaurants and still very popular. Lots of fish dishes, but also good steaks. One of the few restaurants in the city that does not accept reservations – people line up outside and take their chance. $$

Zuni Café & Grill, 1658 Market Street, tel: 552-2522. Classic California cuisine for the Castro District set. Famed for its huge selection of oysters. $$

Marimba, 2317 Chestnut Street, tel: 776-1506. Stylish Mexican restaurant with colorful dolls on the walls and light cuisine on the tables. $–$$

Café Tosca, 242 Columbus Avenue, tel: 986-9651. The place for the Italian-artist set in North Beach. Perfect for a cappuccino. $

Fruit flans with flair

Street food, California style

Campo Santo, 240 Columbus Avenue, tel: 433-9623. The chairs wobble and the ceiling is low, but this is the most popular Mexican restaurant in North Beach. $

Hongkong Teahouse, 835 Pacific Avenue, tel: 391-6365. An atmosphere not unlike Beijing station concourse, but on the trolleys are fine dim sum delicacies. Simple, but cheap. $

The Bean Scene Café, 582 Sutter Street, tel: 433-5525. Nice breakfast café near Union Square. Fresh croissants and excellent bagels with cream cheese to accompany a cup of coffee. $

Napa

Meadowood Restaurant, 900 Meadowood Lane, St Helena, tel: (707) 963-3646. Franco-Californian cuisine in the hotel of the same name.Good views. $$$

All Seasons Café, 1400 Lincoln Avenue, Calistoga, tel: (707) 942-9111. Bistro with excellent wine list and good California cuisine. $$

Tra Vigne, 1050 Charter Oak Avenue, St Helena, tel: (707) 963-444. Italian cuisine. Very popular. $

Monterey

The Charthouse, 444 Cannery Row, tel: (408) 372-3362. Excellent fish and steaks in this famous locale, with a fine view over the Bay. $$

Abalonetti, 57 Fisherman's Wharf, tel:(408) 373-1851. Enjoy lunch on the veranda with a view over the water. Italian cuisine. $

Good for grills

Shopping

Shoppers will find a good choice of shops around **Union Square** and along **Market Street**. Macy's and other department stores are located here, together with smaller fashion retailers, jeans shops, art galleries and antique shops. For top fashions and amusing bric-à-brac, try elegant **Union Street**. Avant-garde art, unusual and off-beat clothing and nostalgic souvenirs from the age of flower power are on sale in **Haight Street** or **Fillmore Street**.

Several smallish shopping centers, such as The Cannery, Pier 39 or Ghirardelli Square are clustered around **Fisherman's Wharf**, selling mainly T-shirts, postcards and knick-knacks. Even among these, however, are some out-of-the ordinary souvenirs: colorful dragons to hang in the wind, unusual toys, bizarre sun-glasses or 'food art', perfect for the next party.

Jeans were invented in San Francisco

Shopping centers

San Francisco Shopping Center, corner of Market Street and Powell Street. A nine-story shopping center with the Nordstrom department store and about 100 other shops. The spiral escalators are a curiosity.

Crocker Galleria, 50 Post Street. Elegant, smallish shopping center with top-class fashion and jewelry shops.

Embarcadero Center, corner of California Street and Market Street. Spacious shopping center in the lower three stories of this high-rise complex.

100 stores in the San Francisco Shopping Center

Department stores

Macy's, corner of Stockton Street and O'Farrell Street. An institution. Sells everything.

Neiman Marcus, 150 Stockton Street. Top fashions, cosmetics and a delicatessen. Good restaurant.

Book and record shops

Sierra Club Bookstore, 730 Polk Street. Maps and walking guides from the famous nature preservation society.

Borders Books, 400 Post Street. San Francisco's biggest bookshop with over 160,000 titles. CDs, videos and an espresso bar.

Harold's Newsstand, 529 Geary Street. International newspapers.

European Book Company, 925 Larkin Street. Foreign-language newspapers and books.

Macy's near Market Street

Paws for a browse

Virgin Megastore, 2 Stockton Street. Gigantic is the only word to describe this 'superstore'. 150,000 CDs for sale.

Rough Trade Records, 1529 Haight Street. Large selection of used CDs and LPs.

Clothes

Sportswear to go

Eddie Bauer, 250 Post Street. Top-class sportswear.

Six Sixty Center, 660 3rd Street. Discount shopping center with about 20 clothes and shoe shops.

Yerba Buena Square, 599 Howard Street. Designer fashion boutique with factory sales at reasonable prices.

Emporio Armani, 1 Grant Street (not the same as **Giorgio Armani**, 278 Post Street). A slightly cheaper version of the exclusive Italian designer. Good-looking premises.

Other shops

Ultimate yogurt

F.A.O. Schwarz, 48 Stockton Street. Branch of the famous New York toyshop. A children's paradise.

Ghirardelli Chocolate Shop, 900 Northpoint Street. San Francisco's best-known chocolate store.

Gump's, 135 Post Street. Long-established store selling jewelry, porcelain and glassware.

S.F. MOMA Museum Store, 151 3rd Street. A huge collection of art books, souvenirs, jewelry and postcards.

Napa Valley Wine Exchange, 415 Taylor Street. California wine, ready-packaged for the journey home.

Nightlife

San Francisco is not especially noted for its frenzied nightlife, but whether it is opera, reggae, techno or musicals that interest you, the city has them, often with top-class performers. **North Beach** has all the traditional night-time attractions, but try **South of Market** for clubs and discos and **Haight-Ashbury** and **Fillmore** for live music and bars.

The nightlife scene is fairly constant with clubs remaining fashionable for several years. To find out what is on where, consult *Datebook* in the weekend edition of the *San Francisco Chronicle* or *SF Weekly*, available free in many music shops and bars.

Into the night

Ticket sales

BASS Tickets, tel: (510) 762-2277. Tickets for every major musical and sporting event in the city. Sales points in Union Square, the Embarcadero Center and several large music shops.

TIX Bay Area, Stockton Street near Union Square, tel: 433-7827. Sale of tickets at half-price for performances on the same evening.

Opera, Ballet and Concerts

War Memorial Opera House, Civic Center, tel: 846-3330. San Francisco's magnificent opera house is closed until the fall of 1997 for renovation work. Themed festivals in the summer, such as the 'Opera Pops' or Wagner festivals. Standing room tickets can be purchased two hours before the performance.

San Francisco Symphony Orchestra, Davies Symphony Hall, tel: 864-6000. Concerts by the city's celebrated symphony orchestra, but guest orchestras and conductors too.

San Francisco Ballet, tel: 865-2000. Classical and modern ballet at the Center for the Arts in the Yerba Buena Gardens and Palace of Fine Arts theater. The *Nutcracker* is always performed around Christmas.

Theater and Musicals

American Conservatory Theater, tel: 749-2228. San Francisco's most famous theater group performs modern plays, as well as Shakespearean classics. The company uses several different stages in the city.

Curran Theater, 445 Geary Street, tel: 776-1999. Small theater that has been showing *Phantom of the Opera* for several years.

Opportunities for opera

A squeeze play

65

Your host for an evening

Bar-room banter

Blind Pig bar, 1904

Orpheum Theater, 1192 Market Street, tel: 776-1999. Various Broadway musicals on the program.

Actors' Theatre, 533 Sutter Street, tel: 296-9179. Often does classics by such luminaries as Tennessee Williams and other dramatists.

The Magic Theater, Fort Mason, Building D, tel: 441-8822. Innovative and known for premiering plays by Michael McClure and Sam Shephard.

Potrero Hill Neighborhood House, 953 De Haro, tel: 826-8080. Professionals and amateurs perform together to present contemporary issues and gritty, urban themes.

Beach Blanket Babylon, Club Fugazi, 678 Green Street, tel: 421-4222. For 20 years, one of the most popular musical revue bars in the city.

Bars

Redwood Room, 495 Geary Street. Nostalgic Art Deco bar in the Clift Hotel with an elegant setting and original Klimt paintings.

View Lounge, 55 4th Street. Bar on the 39th floor of the Marriott Hotel with a fine view over the city. Romantic piano music in the background.

View Bar, Hyatt Regency Embarcadero. Smart rendezvous with city panorama. Opposite the Ferry Building. San Francisco's only revolving bar.

The Red Room, 825 Sutter Street. Trendy bar with a classical 1920s look.

Gordon Biersch Brewery, 2 Harrison Street. Mini-brewery with restaurant and large bar.

San Francisco Brewing Company, 155 Columbus Avenue. One of the oldest small-scale breweries in the city. Fine old dark wood bar.

Washington Square Bar, 1707 Powell Street. Classical-style old bar in the heart of North Beach.

Vesuvio's, 255 Columbus Avenue. Henri Lenoir's bar was a 1950s literary institution.

Dubliner Pub, 3838 24th Street, tel: 826 2279. Friendly neighborhood pub in Noe Valley, run by Dubliner Patrick Kent. London Pride and Bass ales.

Dancing and discos

OZ, Union Square. Elegant dance bar in the Westin St Francis Hotel.

Club DV8, 540 Howard Street. Well-established disco, now a classic in the SoMa quarter.

New DNA Lounge, 375 11th Street. Large dance club for younger clientele with DJs and live bands.

Caesar's Latin Palace, 3140 Mission Street. Traditional Latin and salsa music and shows.

New Orleans Room, Fairmont Hotel, 950 Mason. Hot jazz and swing-era music.

Clubs

The Saloon, 1232 Grant Avenue, tel: 989-7666. Smoky bar popular with blues fans.

Slim's, 333 11th Street, tel: 621-3330. Rock club in the SoMa quarter favored by blues and country fans.

The Great American Music Hall, 859 O'Farrell Street, tel: 885-0750. Classic club in an historic concert hall. Different bands, different types of music most evenings.

Finoccio's, 506 Broadway, tel: 982-9388. Famous for almost 50 years of female impersonators.

Bimbo's 365 Club, 1025 Columbus Avenue, tel: 474-0365. Elegant night club. Changing shows with live acts.

Pier 23, The Embarcadero. Jazz club in an old pier.

Sailors' delight

67

North Beach naughtiness

Getting There and Around

Opposite: California cruising

From the Airport

San Francisco International Airport (SFO) lies on the west bank of the Bay about 12 miles (20km) south of the city center. SFO Airporter buses run every 15 minutes from the airport to the major downtown hotels. Fare: under $10. Supershuttle minibuses (tel: 558-8500) will deliver you to the door of your hotel for between $10 and $12. A taxi will cost in the region of $30. The journey takes about 25 minutes, depending on traffic conditions.

Several domestic carriers also serve **Oakland International Airport**, from where a shuttle takes passengers to the Bay Area Rapid Transit (BART) station for a 30-minute ride to downtown San Francisco. Airport coaches, taxis, and various shuttles provide transportation as well. Some visitors may also arrive at **San Jose International Airport**, also served by a number of domestic airlines and located about an hour south of the downtown area.

The city from the air

Buses, streetcars and cable cars

Compared to many other American cities, San Francisco has an excellent public transportation system. The buses of the **San Francisco Municipal Railway** (MUNI) cover the whole of the city and streetcars run along Market Street. The MUNI also operate the three city-center cable car services: California, Mason and Hyde. The latter two travel up and around from the downtown area to Fisherman's Wharf; California takes a steep but straight line from the Financial District over Nob Hill to the Van Ness corridor. Your ticket is transferable among the routes and also good for the MUNI system. MUNI bus tickets are good on the cable system, but the difference in the fare must be made up to the conductor on boarding. It is easier to use the sidewalk vending machines to get your cable ticket, and you can ride on one ticket on as many routes as you can squeeze into the time period indicated. Be forewarned that the Mason and Hyde lines in particular tend to be very crowded. Plan your time to allow for a wait in line coming back from Fisherman's Wharf.

For information about times and routes, call 673-6864. A route map and economical multi-ticket are available at the Visitors Bureau by Hallidie Plaza. **MUNI Passports** are available for a day, for three days and for seven days. This 'passport' entitles you to reduced admission charges at about 25 museums and tourist sights in the city.

A streetcar is desired

BART

The modern **Bay Area Rapid Transit** (BART) is a 68-mile (110km) suburban commuter railroad network. It mainly serves the towns to the south of San Francisco and on

69

the east side of the Bay. Some sections of track run underground, including the 3½-mile (6km) long Transbay Tube between San Francisco and Oakland. The system is fully automated and all stations (marked with a blue and white sign) have wall maps showing nearby tourist attractions, shopping areas and connecting bus lines. There are displays of printed information explaining station locations, fares and ticket-buying procedures.

Tourists can ride BART for a special reduced fare which entitles you to use the system for up to three hours, but you must enter and exit from the same station. Commuters crowd the cars during the morning and evening rush hours.

Taxis

Given the chronic shortage of parking spaces, taxis are infinitely preferable to renting a car. They are also fairly inexpensive, as distances within the city tend to be short journies. There are hardly any taxi ranks, but you can ask at any hotel or restaurant for a cab to be called. Otherwise, either hail a taxi from the sidewalk in the city center or look for one waiting near the big hotels.

Car rental

If you want to tour the suburbs or a little further afield, a rental car is recommended. If you just want a car for a day or two, you can reserve one through the main companies such as Hertz, Dollar, Alamo, or Avis – they all have branches in downtown San Francisco. Drivers must be 21 years old and possess a valid or international drivers' license. If you are intending to explore more of California, then it is advisable to book your car (or camper van) before leaving home. This often works out much cheaper as fully comprehensive insurance (expensive in California) and unlimited mileage are often included in the package.

Useful information and maps are available from the office of the **American Automobile Association** (AAA, 150 Van Ness Avenue, tel: 565-2012). Do not forget your membership card. The AAA offers reciprocal arrangements with many European clubs.

Ferries

As well as the guided harbor tours *(see page 72)*, the ferries across the Bay offer good sightseeing opportunities. **Golden Gate Ferries** operate from the Ferry Building at the foot of Market Street to Sausalito and Larkspur at the north end of the Bay. The **Blue & Gold Fleet** also leave from the Ferry Building and from Pier 39 to Oakland, Alameda and Vallejo. Ships of the **Red & White Fleet** depart from Pier 43 ½ by Fisherman's Wharf to Sausalito and Tiburon.

Visitors to Pier 39

Facts for the Visitor

Tourist information

Contact your local travel agent for general information and pre-trip documentation. Brochures about California, maps, accommodation addresses and an events calendar can be supplied by the **California Division of Tourism**, PO Box 1499, Dept. 300, Sacramento, CA 95812, tel: (916) 322-2881, fax: 322-3402.

The **San Francisco Convention and Visitors Bureau**, 201 3rd Street, Suite 900, San Francisco, CA 94103-3185, tel: (415) 391-200, fax: 227-2668 will supply specialist information and the latest edition of the 'San Francisco Book' with up-to-date addresses, information and descriptions of the main tourist attractions. The **Visitor Center** in the basement of Hallidie Plaza, 900 Market Street, will also supply literature (Monday to Friday, 9am–5.30pm, Saturday 9am–3pm and Sunday 10am–2pm).

In the smaller towns of central California, the local **Chamber of Commerce** or the **Visitor & Convention Bureaus** can often provide helpful information.

Napa Valley
Napa Valley Visitors Bureau, Napa, 1310 Napa Town Center, tel: (707) 226-7459, fax: 255-2066.

Sonoma Valley
Sonoma Visitors Bureau, 435 First Street E, tel: (707) 938-1266. For maps and addresses of the wineries which offer guided tours and wine tasting.

Monterey
Monterey Peninsula Visitors & ConventionBureau, 380 Alvarado Street, Monterey, tel: (408) 649-1770, fax: 649-3502.

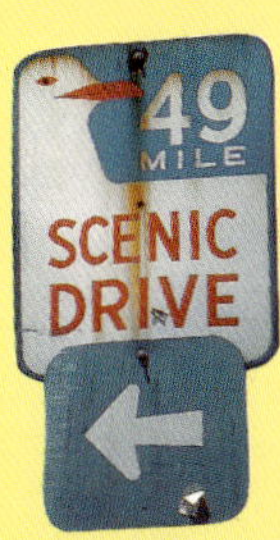

71

The weather encourages outdoor activities

Travel documents

International travelers should bring a valid passport. No visa is required if your length of stay does not exceed 90 days and you can furnish a valid return ticket. If you want to stay longer, apply for a visa at the US Consulate.

The length of stay is determined by the immigration officer you meet on arrival, so it's a good idea to have ready such things as credit cards, traveler's checks or hotel reservation forms if requested to do so.

Customs

Items for personal use can be brought into the US duty-free. Duty-free allowances include 200 cigarettes or 50 cigars or 2kg of tobacco; 1 liter of alcoholic drink and presents to the value of $100. Flowers, meat, vegetables or fruit may not be brought into the country.

Sightseeing tours

By bus

Gray Line of San Francisco, Union Square, Powell Street/Geary Street, tel: 558-9400. One of the biggest companies with a wide range of half-day and whole-day sightseeing tours on buses or converted cable cars with wheels. Also nightlife tours.

Take a sightseeing tour

By air

San Francisco Seaplane Tours, Mill Valley, tel: 332-4843. Tours over San Francisco by seaplane. They leave from Fisherman's Wharf or Sausalito.

By boat

Blue & Gold Fleet, Pier 39, Fisherman's Wharf, tel: 705-5555. Boat trips lasting 75 minutes cruise past the city center to the Golden Gate Bridge. Also dinner cruises.

Red & White Fleet, Piers 41 and 43½, Fisherman's Wharf, tel: 546-2700. One-hour trips across the Bay and tours of Alcatraz (book with credit card on 546-2700).

Rent a bicycle

On foot

Chinatown Adventure Tours, 750 Kearny Street, tel: 355-9657. Two- to four-hour guided tours through Chinatown with a Chinese tea ceremony or dim sum lunch.

Flower-Power Haight-Ashbury Tour, 520 Shrader Street, tel: 221-8442. Two-hour walks through the former hippy neighborhood. Usually Tuesday and Sunday at 9.30am.

The City Guides, Main Library, Civic Center, tel: 557-4266. Charitable body which organizes free guided tours to the main historic and cultural sights.

Tipping

In restaurants, service tends not to be included within the price, but it is usual to leave a sum equivalent to about 15 percent of the bill on the table or to add it to the credit card slip. This sum should not be regarded as a tip but as payment for the service provided. A hotel porter gets about $1–2 for each item of luggage, taxi-drivers and hair-dressers expect 10 to 15 percent of the bill and it is customary to leave the hotel chambermaid $1–2 for each day stayed.

Opening times

Smaller shops are generally open Monday to Saturday from 9 or 10am until 6pm. Department stores and shopping malls around Union Square stay open from 10am to 7pm, but on Thursday and Saturday until 8pm and Sunday 11am to 6pm. Some supermarkets stay open around the clock. Banks open Monday to Friday 9am–3pm, but on one day, either Thursday or Friday, stay open until 6pm. Museums usually open from 10am to 4pm, but many close on Monday.

Public holidays

New Year's Day (January 1); Martin Luther King Day (3rd Monday in January); Presidents' Day (3rd Monday in February); Memorial Day (last Monday in May); Independence Day (July 4); Labor Day (1st Monday in September); Columbus Day (2nd Monday in October); Veterans' Day (November 11); Thanksgiving (4th Thursday in November); Christmas Day (December 25).

Most government offices, museums and post offices are closed on national holidays. Shops and malls in central San Francisco usually stay open, however, and many have gigantic sales at these times.

Hotel guests should tip for any extra services

Shopping hours vary

Chinese New Year lasts for two entire weeks

    If a fixed holiday falls on a Sunday, the following Monday usually counts as the holiday. Many people take short breaks over the Memorial Day and Labor Day weekends, so accommodation, particularly in San Francisco, Monterey and Napa can be difficult to find, unless pre-booked.

Gifts found only in Chinatown

Telephones

The area code for San Francisco is 415. For Oakland and the other towns on the east side of the Bay, the code is 510, although plans are afoot to introduce a series of additional codes throughout California. Making local calls is easy: lift the receiver, insert 25¢ and dial the seven-digit number. To find out the numbers of people or places, dial 411. To make long-distance calls, dial 0 for the operator. Direct dialing is possible if the full area code is known. Overseas calls can also be made by dialing direct, but if you're calling from a pay phone, your pockets will have to be stuffed full of quarters. The code for the UK is 011 44, followed by the area code minus the initial zero; Australia's code is 011 61 and New Zealand's 011 64; for Canada just dial the area code and the number code.

Renting a car is unnecessary

Post offices

Post office are usually open from Monday to Friday, 8.30am–5pm, but stamps are available in souvenir shops, at hotel receptions and at the small postal counters in many supermarkets. The main post office at 150 Steuart Street (at the Bay end of Market Street) is also open from 9am to 2pm. Another central post office is situated at 150 Sutter Street.

Important mail or packages can be sent via private courier services such as 'Federal Express' or 'UPS'. This is an expensive way of sending mail, but two-day delivery times to Europe are guaranteed.

The city is on Pacific Standard Time

Time

Pacific Standard Time applies in California. When it is noon Standard Time in San Francisco, it is 8pm in London. 'Daylight Saving Time', i.e., when clocks are advanced by one hour, applies from the beginning of April to the end of October.

Voltage

110 volts AC. An adapter will be necessary for European electrical appliances such as shavers and hairdryers.

Medical assistance

To find the addresses of doctors, dentists and hospitals, consult the Yellow Pages telephone directory. Medicine is available in the pharmacies on the main shopping streets or at drugstores in large supermarkets. Hospitals with a

24-hour accident and emergency service are the St Francis Memorial Hospital, 900 Hyde Street, tel: 353-6000 and San Francisco General Hospital, 1001 Potrero Avenue, tel: 206-8111.

Emergencies

Within San Francisco, call 911 for the police, fire department, highway patrol or an emergency doctor. Otherwise, contact a telephone operator for emergency help by dialing 0. Money transfers within 24 hours can be arranged by Western Union (see telephone book).

Crime

San Francisco and central California are usually fairly safe destinations but, as in all major cities, you should be vigilant. In the harbor area of south San Francisco, in the run-down Tenderloin district north of City Hall and in the area around Alamo Square, tourists should take great care, particularly at night.

When traveling through the more remote parts of the city, lock your car internally. In Golden Gate Park and near other tourist attractions, never leave anything visible in a parked car. If you get lost in what looks like one of the poorer areas, try to get back on to a main street as quickly as possible.

Alcohol

As a rule, alcoholic drinks (and that includes beer) are only sold to anyone age 21 or over and identity card checks in clubs and bars are usually made. Beer and wine may be bought in food stores, but stronger drinks are available only in liquor stores.

It is an offense to drink alcohol in a car. Open bottles must be kept in the trunk.

Ask a policeman

75

Meander through the Maritime Museum

Sonoma's Swiss Hotel

Abigail Hotel

Marriott Hotel

Where to Stay

The hotel trade in San Francisco has a long tradition. During the last century, as well as all the adventurers in search of gold, thousands of bankers and businessmen arrived who were not prepared to live in tents. Luxurious hotels appeared on Nob Hill and dozens of smaller hotels were constructed around Union Square. These delightful, five- to ten-story structures with iron fire escapes on the front are typical of San Francisco. Many have recently been renovated and furnished either in traditional or ultra-modern style.

As well as these older hotels, all the international chains have a presence in the city, often in vast steel and glass towers. Non-smoking rooms, sometimes non-smoking floors, are common. Increasingly, hotels are adopting a 'no smoking policy' that applies to all rooms.

Although in theory there are some 30,000 hotel rooms in San Francisco, it is a good idea to book accommodation in advance, especially around Easter, in the middle of summer and in the fall. On public holidays, a reservation is essential. If you do not book through a travel agent, then you will have to give a credit card number to secure the room until your arrival.

Hotel selection

The following suggestions are listed according to three categories: $$$ = expensive (from $150); $$ = moderate ($80–150); $ = inexpensive (up to $80).

San Francisco
Fairmont, 950 Mason Street, CA 94108, tel: 772-5000, fax: (415) 772-5013. The Fairmont, on Nob Hill, opened in 1902 as the best hotel in town. Despite the loss of some

of its splendor, it is still a legend and a whiff of nostalgia blows through its lobbies and 536 rooms. The view over the city from the top floors is simply marvelous. $$$.

Hyatt Regency Embarcadero, 5 Embarcadero Center, CA 94111, tel: (415) 788-1234, fax: 981-3638. This large, futuristic hotel at the Bay end of Market Street is reminiscent of the *Starship Enterprise*, but the 803 rooms are very comfortably furnished. $$$.

Hyatt Regency

The Marriott Hotel, 55 4th Street, CA 94103, tel: (415) 896-1600, fax: 896-6176. The hotel's mirrored green-glass exterior, looking from a distance like a giant juke-box, is a local landmark. $$$.

Hotel Diva, 440 Geary Street, CA 94102, tel: (415) 885-0200, fax: 346-6613. The Diva is the creation of well-known designers, right down to the last detail. All 108 rooms are different, some very colorfully decorated. The lobby area has a hi-tech look that goes well with the young clientele. $$–$$$.

The Mark Hopkins, One Nob Hill, CA 94108, tel: (415) 392-3434, fax: 421-3302. A fine hotel at the top of Nob Hill. Elegantly renovated and impeccable service. Many of the rooms in the 17-story building have a magnificent view. Panoramic view from the restaurant. $$$.

Mark Hopkins Hotel

The Warwick Regis, 490 Geary Street, CA 94102, tel: (415) 928-7900, fax: 441-8788. Pleasant, old, nicely restored hotel. The 74 rooms are modern and functionally furnished. Continental breakfasts served. $$–$$$.

The Abigail Hotel, 246 McAllister Street, CA 94103, tel: (415) 861-9728, fax: 861-5848. Good value and conveniently located near the Civic Center, this small 60-room hotel, which was built in the 1920s for visiting theater troupes, has a cozy, arty ambience. $.

Best Western Americana, 121 7th Street, CA 94130, tel: (415) 626-0200, fax: 626-3974. Architecturally unusual motel near South of Market. Colorful facade and a palm-lined inner courtyard with swimming pool. The 142 rooms are bright and spacious. $$.

Hotel Bohème, 444 Columbus Avenue, CA 94133, tel: (415) 433-9111, fax: 362-6292. A small artists' hotel in North Beach, rather like a Parisian pension. The 15 rooms are tastefully decorated with modern art. Casual atmosphere with friendly, young and helpful staff who can supply good advice about the nightlife. $$.

Hotel Beresford, 635 Sutter Street, CA 94102, tel: (415) 673-9900, fax: 474-0449. Very comfortable mid-range hotel near Union Square. Tastefully renovated.$$.

Red Victorian Peace Center B&B, 1665 Haight Street, CA 94117, tel: (415) 864-1978, fax: 863-3293. Light-hearted B&B hotel in the Haight-Ashbury area. Relive the 1960s here. Every room is different, sometimes ultra-modern, sometimes reflective, sometimes flower power.$$.

The Fitzgerald

The Fitzgerald, 620 Post Street, CA 94109, tel: (415) 775-8100, fax: 775-1278. Beautifully restored, elegant hotel near Union Street with 45 bright, spacious rooms.$$.

The Orchard, 562 Sutter Street, CA 94102, tel: (415) 433-4434, fax: 433-3695. Dating from 1906, this is now in the luxury class category. Top-class service.$$.

Commodore Hotel, 825 Sutter Street, CA 94109 tel: (415) 923-6800, fax: 923-6804. Stylish nostalgia in one of the prettiest of the renovated hotels of the1920s. All 113 rooms have designer furnishings.$-$$.

78

San Remo Hotel, 2237 Mason Street, CA 94133, tel: (415) 776-8688, fax: 776-2811. Built near Fisherman's Wharf in 1906 as a hostel for workers and earthquake victims, it is now an unusual hotel, favored by young Europeans. Few of the rooms have their own bath.$.

Napa
Silverado Country Club, 1600 Atlas Peak Road, Napa, tel: (707) 257-0200, fax: 257-5407. Spacious golf and tennis resort hotel at the southern end of the valley.$$$.

Best Western Napa Valley Lodge, 2230 Madison Street, Yountville, tel: (707) 944-2468, fax: 944-9362. Good looking mid-range hotel in the heart of the valley.$$.

Sonoma
Swiss Hotel, 18 West Spain Street, Sonoma, tel: (707) 938 2884. This tiny (five guest rooms) B & B with views overlooking the plaza has been an inn since 1909. $$-$$$.

Monterey: Cannery Row

Monterey
Monterey Plaza Hotel, 400 Cannery Row, tel: (408) 646-1700, fax: 646-5937. First-class hotel at the heart of Cannery Row. Part of the building hangs over the water.$$$.

Casa Munras, 700 Munras Avenue, tel: (408) 375-2411, fax: 375-1365. On the edge of the old town. Nice gardens and large balconies.$$.

PIER 39
HARASSMENT OF
SEA LIONS IS
A VIOLATION OF
THE MARINE
MAMMAL
PROTECTION ACT
'NO DOCKING'